Television and Repetition

I0123741

Resisting some of the negative connotations that repetition can attract, this book illustrates how it has been used as a catalyst for creative expression across a range of television genres.

Divided into two parts, the first three chapters contextualise repetition within related media and critical debates, before locating it as an important facet of television that is worth exploring in detail. The final three chapters discuss specific television shows that incorporate repetition creatively within their narrative structure and aesthetic composition, ranging from *The Royle Family* and *Doctor Who* to *I May Destroy You* and *This is Going to Hurt*. In each case, James Walters argues that repetition emerges as crucial to the expression of key themes and ideas, thus becoming a structural and compositional element itself.

Exploring the ways in which repetition has featured in the work of figures such as Umberto Eco, Raymond Bellour and Bruce Kawin, and has influenced the approaches of television scholars like Raymond Williams, Roger Silverstone and John Ellis, this book is essential reading for scholars and students of film, television and media studies.

James Walters is Reader in Film and Television Studies at the University of Birmingham. He is the author and editor of many books in these fields, and his work has appeared in numerous collections and academic journals.

Television and Repetition

James Walters

R Routledge
Taylor & Francis Group

LONDON AND NEW YORK

First published 2024
by Routledge
4 Park Square, Milton Park, Abingdon, Oxon OX14 4RN

and by Routledge
605 Third Avenue, New York, NY 10158

Routledge is an imprint of the Taylor & Francis Group, an informa business

© 2024 James Walters

British Library Cataloguing-in-Publication Data
A catalogue record for this book is available from the British Library

ISBN: 978-1-032-20797-1 (hbk)
ISBN: 978-1-032-20798-8 (pbk)
ISBN: 978-1-003-26528-3 (ebk)

DOI: 10.4324/9781003265283

Typeset in Times New Roman
by MPS Limited, Dehradun

Contents

Figures

Acknowledgements

The gestation period for this book has been relatively lengthy and has changed form in various ways during that time. It began some time ago and included an article I wrote for a collection co-edited by my colleague Rob Stone (*The Routledge Companion to World Cinema*). I am very grateful to Rob for that opportunity to kick things off, and for the generous encouragement and enthusiasm, he has shown for this project over the years. The University of Birmingham continues to provide a lively and supportive environment for pursuing research, and I am especially lucky to have such wonderful colleagues in the Department of Film and Creative Writing. I owe a debt of gratitude to the excellent team at Routledge, especially Kelly O'Brien and Natalie Foster, not only for their dedicated guidance but also for remarkable patience when, for example, I decided that this book should be about television rather than film (after the contract had been signed and writing had begun). I would like to thank my wife, Amy, and my boys, Isaac, Ruben, Fergus, and Milo, for all the love and happiness they bring to my life, and for putting up with all my distracted responses as I was buried in reading or tapping away at the laptop. Finally, and unfortunately, some of the research and writing for the book had to be undertaken in various locations within the oncology wards at the Leicester Royal Infirmary. I'm not sure any words could adequately express my gratitude to the staff for the expert care they provide in such exceptionally difficult circumstances, so I simply dedicate this book to them.

Introduction

There are countless themes and interests that can find a place within the study of television. This book takes repetition as its central focus and, in doing so, aims to look at this aspect in a little more detail than might previously have been afforded. That could be interpreted as a suggestion that repetition has been unfairly overlooked or neglected. However, I would not want to suggest that there is any special reason why repetition might be explored above and beyond other important areas in television studies that *have* received attention. Indeed, I can think of reasons why repetition might be overlooked or perhaps even avoided. Repetition carries with it certain negative associations: tedium, monotony, limitation, a lack of invention or originality, for example. Before publishing his seminal text, *TV: The Most Popular Art* (1974), Horace Newcomb wrote another paper entitled: 'The Problem of Repetition in Television.' Newcomb summarises his argument by explaining that: 'I essentially said that I didn't like these stories that repeat themselves all the time' (McPherson 2007). It is intriguing that a figure like Newcomb's starting point in television studies should concern something he didn't favour, and it is significant that he should so readily and overtly identify repetition as fundamentally problematic. The paper was delivered as a spoken text and never published, with Newcomb finding encouragement to pursue a different direction (soap opera, at the time). I suspect his view of repetition would not have been uncommon (although the decision to address the topic directly self-evidently was) and, had it been disseminated more widely, might have elicited favourable, perhaps even widespread, agreement. Perceptions may not have shifted dramatically since. Writing at the end of the 1960s, Newcomb is concerned with television content and his assertion is that shows offer the same thing again and again, but we might easily couple this with adverse responses to repeated programming within television schedules more broadly (which chapter two of this books attends to in greater detail). I would suggest that neither view is extinct today and that viewers are still resistant to the

DOI: 10.4324/9781003265283-1

idea of sameness, even when we seek out repeated content for pleasure or comfort, as many did when revisiting familiar television shows during the pandemic-enforced lockdowns of 2020 (Bryan 2020).

This is not to say that repetition is unequivocally cherished in other media. Writing about cinema at the turn of the century, David Sanjek remarks that: 'The profusion of sequels, remakes, and narratives that amalgamate familiar elements into various forms of pastiche results perhaps not in contempt on the part of consumers, but a weariness bred of sensory overload and intellectual understimulation' (Sanjek 2000, 111). Clearly, for Sanjek, the very fact that a film might be viewed as a repetition of pre-existing content would associate it with a lack of quality and ambition. This opinion is not uncommon and arguably intensified in the twenty-first century as the proliferation of titles in series such as Star Wars, Harry Potter, Transformers, and Marvel coincided with the birth of social media critique. Indeed, the first chapter of this book will touch briefly upon film franchises, which are often discussed in this manner and certainly offer instances of elaborate repetition. Yet, television seems notable for the way in which repetition can infuse its content very specifically and its form more broadly, with neither type necessarily offering a cause for celebration among audiences. Perhaps this unfavourable view of repetition in television has been reinforced inadvertently in academic debate as scholarship on television has quite understandably tended to praise works that embody innovation and originality. As critical writing has, throughout the twenty-first century, placed greater emphasis on quality and achievement in television,[1] it is hardly surprising that repetition should not have become a guiding concern. And, of course, television has hardly enjoyed an unblemished reputation. Charlotte Brunsdon has reflected insightfully upon a transition in language from the 'widespread characterisation of regular [television] viewing as an addiction' to the 'emergence of the somatic metaphor of "bingeing" to describe the domestic viewing of multiple episodes sequentially' that effectively replaces the view of 'an involuntary, non-cerebral relation to the medium, an out of control habit' with 'connotations of an uncontrollable, excessive consumption' (Brunsdon 2010, 64–65). Consequently, the move from 'addiction' to 'bingeing' retains similarly negative appraisals of the fundamental act of television viewing, regardless of the type of content these terms tend to be associated with (soap opera and prestige drama, respectively, in Brunsdon's argument). The combination of repetition *and* television might therefore represent a somewhat unappealing prospect.

This book exists partially in response to the rather negative perceptions of repetition and television and, perhaps relatedly, the relative neglect those two subjects have received in combination. The first three chapters will consider these topics more broadly, with the aim of contextualising repetition within related media and critical debates, before locating it as an important facet of television that is worth exploring in detail. The final three chapters will seek to discuss specific television shows that incorporate repetition creatively within their narrative structure and aesthetic composition. In each case, I suggest, repetition emerges as crucial to the expression of key themes and ideas, thus becoming a structural and compositional element itself. There is no attempt, I hope, to propose an overarching theory of repetition in television or to suggest that the shows discussed are most usefully defined by their resemblance to one another within a wider framework. Rather, I intend to emphasise each show's particular employment of repetition so that, even when they are grouped together within a shared thematic focus (as two examples are in each of the final three chapters), they should nevertheless retain their distinctiveness and individuality. This might go some way to countering Newcomb's original suggestion that television offers the same stories, told in the same way, and proposes implicitly that, rather than being regarded only as a problem, repetition in television might instead be appreciated and valued.

Note

1 Jason Jacobs and Steve Peacock's 2013 collection, *Television Aesthetics and Style*, is representative of this trend, and brings together several writers that have contributed to its growth.

1 Approaching Repetition

This book's central concern will be the relationship between television and ideas of repetition. As a consequence, this interest occupies the majority of the work. However, there are also advantages in thinking across boundaries, taking in different art forms, as a means of potentially drawing out and crystallising certain notions relating to repetition that will help to inform some of the directions and perspectives this book will adopt. At one level, this simply reinforces an obvious point that no theme is restricted to any one medium, and that making something like television a main focus is not to implicitly recommend its elevated relevance. Even when one path is chosen, a myriad of legitimate alternatives may equally remain. Moreover, approaching a theme or interest from different angles at the outset might also open out a useful space to think through some aspects of its form and nature, thus keeping the boundaries of debate fairly wide before a stronger emphasis is placed on a specific area (in this case, television).

Repetition and Playing

The screen is dark but, already, a coloured geometric shape made of blocks is falling steadily on its vertical path. At the touch of a button, the shape can be rotated or moved from left to right, but nothing will stop or slow its progress. Finally, it lands at the bottom of the screen, now motionless, rooted into its final resting position. The moment it settles, however, a new geometric shape appears at the top of the screen and begins its own gradual descent. The form of this shape is different from the first but shares the same right-angled block construction. It, too, can be rotated or moved. When it nears the completion of its descent, it can be set apart from the original block, placed alongside it, or fitted against it in tessellation. As its own journey completes, a new shape appears at the top of the screen and begins to fall. When the shapes accumulate and combine at the foot of the screen, they occasionally form complete horizontal lines of blocks, which disappear, creating space for yet more geometric shapes as they continue to fall.

DOI: 10.4324/9781003265283-2

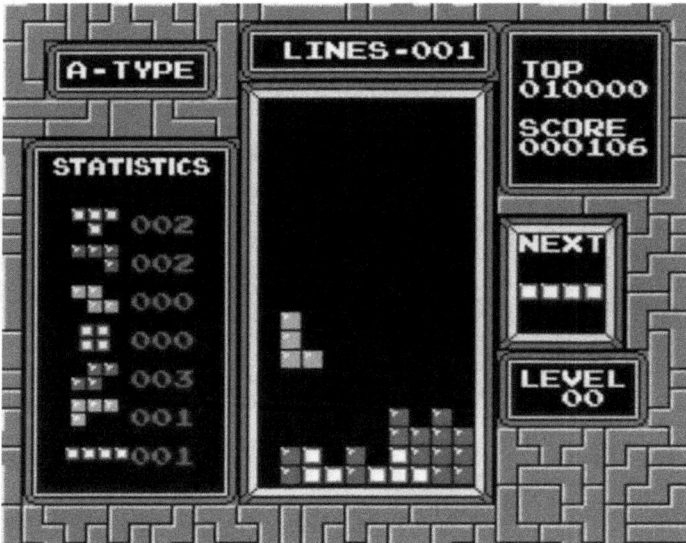

Figure 1.1 Tetris.

In a hotel dining room, a top table has been laid for a wedding reception. Cutlery, crockery, and glassware are arranged in place settings, the folds of the white linen tablecloth bedecked with the pinprick sparkles of festive lights. Seated in an obtuse semicircle in front of the table are four female musicians, dressed in black. Three hold violins in one hand, the necks of the instruments pointing up-right, with bows poised in the other. A fourth, sitting on the right, leans the weight of a cello against her frame, holding it by the neck with a bow in her right hand. The cellist begins first and eight crotchets sound out: D major; A major; B minor; F sharp minor; G major; D major; G major; A major. She plays the sequence a second time and is joined by the violinist seated furthest to the right. On a third playing, the violinist seated second from the right joins them. On the fourth cycle, the final violinist takes up her bow and joins the ensemble. As the quartet play together, the music develops in shape and tone: melodies and countermelodies intertwining to complement and contrast with each other. Finally, the piece slows and ends on a single D major note played in unison. Throughout its duration, the cellist has played the same eight notes over and over in sequence: D major; A major; B minor; F sharp minor; G major; D major; G major; A major.

Figure 1.2 Pachelbel's Canon.

The two events described are the video game *Tetris* and a YouTube performance of Pachelbel's Canon in D Major.[1] They are linked by the theme of repetition and, taken together, have the potential to provide some initial insights into that term and what we might take it to mean. *Tetris* was created by Soviet software engineer Alexey Pajitnov in 1984 and has since enjoyed staggering popularity across global territories. In the game, a player must continue to clear the 'completed' horizontal lines and fill the vacated space with new lines. The game is lost when the playing field is full and no new space can be created. Pachelbel's Canon was largely forgotten since its composition in the early 1680s but enjoyed a revival following a 1968 recording by the Jean-François Paillard chamber orchestra and is now a popular choice at public occasions: notably, wedding ceremonies (Levine 2019).

Even the slightest consideration of the two works reveals their intrinsic connections to the theme of repetition: the incessant falling blocks of *Tetris* and the recurrent bass part of Pachelbel's Canon. However, it is also the case that each illustrates an essential fusion that exists at an equally intrinsic level between repetition and variation. In *Tetris*, the falling geometric objects are not the same each time and, indeed, the purpose of the game is to demand that a player inventively fit together pieces that differ in shape and size. This interaction between player and game necessarily introduces further layers of variance, as not only are the geometric shapes different from each other but they can also be manipulated within the space: moved from side to side, rotated or even accelerated. As a consequence, we are presented with an activity that possesses characteristic repetition but, at the same time, is counterweighted by degrees of variation in its design and execution. This relationship between repetition and variation likewise becomes an essential feature of Pachelbel's Canon. Whilst its inherent repeating is certainly emphasised by the cyclical eight-note structure of the bass part, this quality sits in harmonious tension with the melodies and countermelodies that run over that recurring line, driving the piece in new expressive directions and creating fresh points of resonance and distinction. In this sense, we might be led to propose that the Canon features the tethered foundation of repetition alongside the unfettered freedom of variation in its musical form.

Senses of Repetition

The examples of *Tetris* and Pachelbel's Canon illustrate in relatively straightforward ways the extent to which repetition is very often coupled with variation, to the degree that forms and activities which ostensibly invite the adoption of repetition as a defining characteristic in fact provide an exhibition of the tensions and balances that are created between repetition and variation in their symbiotic relationship to one another. This becomes a concern for the ways in which we employ terminology and, in turn, how precisely the language we adopt describes the appearance, our experience, and our understanding of things. We can explore this issue in slightly more detail if we imagine, for a moment, that *Tetris* and Pachelbel's Canon adopted yet more limited forms and ones which might apparently conform more squarely to a definition of repetition. It is possible to conceive of a version of *Tetris*, for example, in which the descending geometric shape was always the same and could not be manipulated through player interaction. The purpose of the game is, of course, profoundly compromised in this formulation, as the shapes merely stack up on top of each other until their tower can be added to no more. Perhaps, then, a further modification removes the game element completely: the identical shapes do not accumulate at the bottom of the screen but, instead, each one simply disappears as a new shape appears at the top. We might want to say that, with the principles of the game effectively killed off, *Tetris* now responds more directly to the term 'repetition.' And yet, even as geometrically identical shapes fall pointlessly on their vertical path, one after the other, they are still not *exact* repetitions. Each shape forms part of a series that is essentially progressive and so the moment of one shape descending is inherently different from the moment of the previous or the next shape doing likewise. Furthermore, as the shapes fall, the world around them changes and so their activity can never represent exact repetitions within that wider context. If we are witnessing the process, we change as it progresses: our thoughts and behaviours will be altered (becoming influenced by boredom, perhaps) and we are different people, however marginally, from one moment to the next. As a consequence, repetition of this kind can never achieve absolute replication.

Similarly, we might conceive of a hypothetical version of Pachelbel's Canon in which the violin parts were never included and, instead, the piece is comprised entirely of the repeating eight-note bass section. Again, we could perceive this to be a more direct reaction to the concept of repetition, yet the sounding of each note from cycle to cycle would not be identical. There would be minuscule distinctions in the playing of the notes as the bow makes contact with the strings of the instrument in ways that are distinct at an infinitesimal physical level: very slight changes in force, pressure or timing, for example. Consequently, a truly identical note is never guaranteed to be played twice. Additionally, as with the imagined reconfiguration of *Tetris*, the world would not remain the same between each repeating cycle of notes, so each playing occurs within a context that is always changing, rendering exact repetition impossible. As we change, our relationship to our world changes, our relationship to the musical performance changes, and so on.

Umberto Eco considers these kinds of distinctions when attending to the idea of replicas. He asserts that:

> Two sheets of typewriter paper are both *replicas* of the same commercial *type*. In this sense one thing is the same as another when the former exhibits the same properties as the latter, at least under a certain description: two sheets of typing paper are the same from the point of view of our functional needs, even though they are not the same for a physicist interested in the molecular structure of the objects. From the point of view of industrial mass production, two "tokens" can be considered as "replicas" of the same "type" when for a normal person with normal requirements, in the absence of evident imperfection, it is irrelevant whether one chooses one instead of the other. Two copies of a film or of a book are replicas of the same type.
>
> (Eco [1985] 2005, 195)

Here, Eco succinctly describes the kinds of concessions we make in using the terminology of replicas and types, and the extent to which our everyday understanding is necessarily broad and imprecise rather than being motivated by an insistence upon exact replication at a molecular level, for example, which would self-evidently be a practical impossibility for his 'normal person with normal requirements.' In his discussion, Eco connects these contentions to the definition of a 'repeat' and, indeed, we might appreciate the ways in which our use of a term like 'repetition' is similarly broad and imprecise. Indeed, as we justifiably avoid any search for precise replication, we dedicate ourselves to a *sense* of repetition: a feeling that objects, events or activities possess repeated qualities, even if they will almost always lack the exactitude of true repetition.

We might recognise that tension between a sensation or 'feeling' and any insistence on absolute precision in Raymond Bellour's reflections on repetition in relation to cinema. Bellour's intention, in a short article translated for publication in the British journal *Screen* in 1979, is to outline the 'various meanings of the word "repetition" in the specific area of film (films) and cinema' (Bellour 1979, 65). Although the discussion, characteristically for Bellour's writing at the time, arrives ultimately at the then-fashionable (certainly in the pages of *Screen*) area of Metz-influenced semiotic theory, Bellour nevertheless begins with some examples that do not bear the hallmarks of that interest as strongly. His first example of 'external representation' concerns the process of rehearsing and consequently obtaining different takes in filmmaking. On the one hand, Bellour states uncomplicatedly that rehearsals are repetitions (by simply placing the latter term in parenthesis following the first) but then, on the other, he is careful to assert that variation is also a significant feature of rehearsal and, therefore, the production of multiple takes:

> Nevertheless, the variations of the take are just as variable in their *nature*: as much by their numerous paradigms, willingly or unwillingly put into play (framing, lighting etc.) as by these more or less subtle variations of the same thing which, in the fiction film, strive to catch the actor's expression in order to hold that discontinuous moment of eternity that will be indelibly fixed in the thread (film) of representation.
>
> (Ibid, 65-66)

What Bellour seems to acknowledge here is that something like rehearsals and the acquisition of ostensibly similar takes might generally be termed as 'repetition' – may even feel like, or generate a sense of repetition in our considerations, and might even be experienced as such by those involved in the process. But these processes are not, strictly, repetitions: each filmed recapitulation of the material inevitably containing minuscule changes, corresponding with Eco's concept of the replica, discussed earlier but made more visible as we could potentially identify some of the changes that occur between takes, if they were shown in sequence and we were gifted the opportunity to scrutinise them in appropriately close detail, for example. (Perhaps a clearer illustration of this can be found in the existence of continuity errors that occasionally occur in the editing of films, whereby small differences exist between the different takes that have been intercut with each other in the construction of continuous action.) Bellour usefully encapsulates the central tension at work in his phrase 'subtle variations of the same thing,' which alludes to the notion that a group of recorded moments may appear identical (hence, 'the same thing') but will, in fact, display very slight differences (hence, 'subtle variations').

Bellour continues with these thematic concerns when he turns his attention to a second form of external cinematic repetition: the conditions of exhibition. Although acknowledging that the film constitutes a printed text, unlike the relatively ephemeral conditions of theatrical or musical performance, he observes that:

> The quality of the print of a film varies according to the conditions under which the print is struck; in particular it is subject to permanent deterioration, which makes its reproduction the very moment of its material destruction. Screening conditions, on the other hand, are in themselves infinitely variable: from the slight variations between cinemas within one distribution circuit, to massive variations involved in the transition from one format to another (35mm, 16mm, super 8) or even more clearly through a transformation of the medium and of certain of the material conditions of the cinematic apparatus, as is the case with films shown on television.
>
> (Ibid, 66)

Bellour's important point here is that, although we may readily and comfortably talk about having seen the same film as someone else, so alluding to an experience replicated across audiences, changes in aspects like screening conditions and format can subtly but significantly alter that experience from group to group, meaning that we may not be watching the 'same' film in absolute terms at all. Again, it is not difficult to see the connection here with the contrast between having an impression of repetition and experiencing something that is precise repetition. Bellour's points hold when we consider the advancement of exhibition technologies, whereby audiences may not only encounter variable screening conditions in 'traditional' cinemas but also may view those films on televisions with differing visual and audio qualities (different picture features and sizes, as well as different sound systems), mobile devices of varying standards that can possess significantly distinct specifications, for example. Thus, as technology progresses and offers a greater set of viewing opportunities, the notion of film viewing as a repeated experience that occurs uncomplicatedly or inherently between different audiences becomes ever more precarious, underlining and providing an extension to Bellour's reasoning.

Finally, we might attend to Bellour's first example of 'Internal Repetition,' which concerns the film frame. He describes this as:

> An endless repetition, twenty four time per second. But this repetition is, of course, paradoxical. Once on the editing table or on the rewinding table, when the film is severed from its unfolding-purpose, one thing becomes obvious straightaway: the perpetual oscillation,

from one frame to another, between a minute or zero difference and a more marked difference.

(Ibid)

There is perhaps cause to query Bellour's notion that there could ever be 'zero difference' between film frames, even as they occur at twenty-four per second, given that even one twenty-fourth of a second will possess some minuscule distinctions from the next twenty-fourth of a second and the one that preceded it (a more acute example of the kinds of points I raised earlier regarding the 'repetitive' sounding of the bass note in Pachelbel's canon). Nevertheless, his wider point still holds: were we to examine closely the frames on a roll of film, the differences between frames would become apparent, and so any sense that the 'persistence of vision' effect of film projection is achieved through a process of repetition is compromised fundamentally. As Bellour notes, the 'repetition ... is paradoxical.' Here, again, we are touching upon the contrast that exists between generalised or inexact perceptions of repetition and the evidence of variation that can be detected through more precise and exacting examination of the artefacts offered for discussion, whether that is Eco's sheets of typing paper or Bellour's film reels, screenings or takes. The language we use to describe a sensation of repetition may feel comfortable or correct but, in fact, offers an imprecise account of the processes that are actually at work, and whose key characteristic can equally be variation.

Bruce Kawin attends to the distinction between exactitude and imprecision when he is reflecting upon the nature of repetition in literature. In setting up the concerns of his book, *Telling It Again and Again*, he explains that:

> The growth of the work, even from one identical line to another, makes exact repetition impossible: and this, in a sense, is my point. This book is really about the aesthetics of near-repetition. Repetition is a nonverbal state; it cannot be committed to any art that occurs in time. Near-repetition – which, given the strictures of advancing time and linear syntax, is the most that can be done in words or notes or frames – succeeds by intimating, and to a greater or lesser degree almost by containing, the nature of this necessarily nonverbal state.
>
> (Kawin 1972, 7)

Kawin's argument anticipates a discussion of repetition in terms of its aesthetic presentation, which is the focus of his study and which this book will attend to in due course. Nevertheless, his point that the progress of a work is also growth is crucial, creating a logical foundation for the claim that the thing we understand to be and describe as 'repetition' is almost guaranteed to be 'near-repetition,' in his words. In accepting this fact, we should surely find little cause to be troubled by it: it is hardly unusual for everyday colloquial definitions to possess generalised qualities, and this does not necessarily diminish their usefulness or their potency. Kawin's work does not advocate for the replacement of 'repetition' with 'near-repetition' in discussions and, instead, merely asks that we acknowledge certain meanings and understandings that are embedded in our uses of 'repetition' as a descriptive term. More importantly, acknowledging such breadth and imprecision might lead to a profitable reflection upon the ways in which the theme of repetition is evoked within works and the extent to which the tone, style, and mood of evocations – unburdened by the demands of exactitude – can respond to the generalised sensation of repetition that we experience in our lives. Such concerns will inform the progression of the debate within this book.

It is apparent, then, that ideas of repetition are flexible, that the term itself can encompass different notions, and that the pursuit of any definitive singular meaning would by no means constitute a straightforward undertaking. Repetition can also be a feature that occurs not only within a text but also across the wider environments in which that text is found. As discussed, *Tetris* possesses an inherently repetitive form but it is also the case that there is no solitary version of *Tetris* that we can refer to or even claim as a definitive version. Rather, there are numerous official and unofficial versions of the game that spread across many different video gaming platforms. (Indeed, *Tetris* holds a world record for the most ported video game globally.) This proliferation is indicative of a situation whereby a game defined by aspects of repetitive play provides the catalyst for yet wider structures of repetition as *Tetris* is replicated to a dramatic extent, over and over again. In this respect, we might suggest that it constitutes a case of both textual and extratextual repetition. A similar condition can be found in relation to Pachelbel's Canon. Its effective rediscovery in 1968 has led to a vast number of recordings of the piece itself, which is not uncommon for a composition that finds a degree of popularity with a wider public. However, the musical structure of the Canon has also been incorporated continually into other popular music compositions, with the eight-note bass line often featuring prominently.[2] As a result, Pachelbel's work has become a recurring element across many different songs; its repeating form being heard again and again within a wider and expanding pattern of recapitulation. Like *Tetris*, the Canon thus becomes characterised not only by its textual relationship to notions of repetition but also by a process of wider extra-textual repetition as its form is recaptured and reconjured throughout a range of musical reworkings.

Repetition and Recognition

It becomes clearer, through the kinds of relatively detailed considerations undertaken thus far, that this relationship between repetitions that occur within a text and those found externally is evident across a whole range of arts forms. Returning to cinema, for example, cycles of genres can result in overarching patterns of repetition, as groups of titles are produced that share common features. As Lerger Grindon points out, a cycle is: 'a series of genre films produced during a limited period of time and linked by a dominant trend in their use of the genre's conventions. A cycle is often sparked by a benchmark hit, a prototype that is imitated, refined, or resisted by those that follow' (Grindon 2012, 44). Accordingly, film genre cycles may result in examples that repeat certain conventions between themselves but where repetition does not necessarily constitute a defining characteristic of each individual film. Stanley (Stan) Laurel and Oliver (Ollie) Hardy featured in their own highly successful cycle of film comedies that spanned four decades from the 1920s onwards, comprising over one hundred titles, and whose longevity was dependent upon the pair's capacity to continue working and the appetite for that work among audiences and studios. It is certainly the case that routines, catchphrases, and devices were repeated across these films, defining Laurel and Hardy's particular brand of comedy and, at the same time, developing an overarching pattern of repetition within their work. Against this context, their celebrated 1932 film *The Music Box* (Hal Roach) can be seen to possess certain significant qualities.

The story concerns the duo's efforts to deliver a piano to a house sitting at the top of an especially long flight of steps. They are thwarted in their attempts due to a series of mishaps, with a recurring catastrophe being the piano tumbling back down the steps and landing at the bottom. As with *Tetris* and Pachelbel's Canon, even a sparse description of *The Music Box* begins inevitably to reveal some of the repetitions that are inherent within its structure. At one point, however, Stan and Ollie have apparently succeeded in getting the piano to the summit and can deliver it to the property. Reaching the top has involved further calamity, however, as the extensive flight of steps aligns with a smaller run of steps leading up to a pool and fountain sitting in front of the house. Ollie mistakes this new structure for a continuation and, back turned away from his journey as he heaves the piano, thinking he is simply completing their ascent of the main steps, he walks backward into the water. They get the piano back on track and, under Ollie's instruction, position it in front of the house. Ollie walks to the front door and rings the bell pull. Unseen by him, Stan has followed and now stands at his side. Behind them, with no one to secure it, the piano rolls gently out of the frame and back towards the flight of steps. Stan spots this but responds by tapping Ollie on the shoulder to alert him. The pair run after the piano as it pivots back down the steps and makes its clanging descent to the bottom. Ollie somehow gets to it first and grabs hold, but the piano merely pulls him down the steps with it: a wider shot revealing his prostrate form as he is dragged behind, his cries mingling with the discordant ringing of notes spilling out from the instrument. Stan remains on the steps and looks on with mild curiosity, even rising casually on his tiptoes to get a better look. His calmness is contrasted with Ollie's pain and exasperation as he lands at the foot of the steps. He slowly drags himself to a sitting position, grimacing at the painful movement of his aching limbs, pushing up awkwardly on his forearms and sharply kicking out his legs to get there. As he shuffles into position on the pavement and flops his hand down into his lap in frustration, Ollie sighs and looks directly into the camera.

Figure 1.3 The Music Box.

This moment of direct address is not uncommon in Laurel and Hardy's work and, indeed, the look to the camera was a hallmark of Hardy's comic performance, recurring in several of their films. In one sense, it successfully conveys Ollie's frustration at events: utterly perplexed by the world around him, he finds he temporarily has no resources left to contend with it, and so selects a focus outside of his world: the audience beyond the screen. It is possible to contemplate the moment from *The Music Box* a little more closely, however, and consider whether this especially intimate form of engagement might possess further resonances. Ollie's gazing at us seems to reference the particularity of the situation he finds himself in. The piano has once again returned to the foot of the stairs, just as it has done before, its journey made all the more pronounced given that just seconds earlier it was sitting at the top of the summit, ready to be delivered. Any frustration, then, is bound up within the inherent repetition that the film adopts as its defining structure, and which Ollie has become caught up in. As he looks out at us, he steps partially out of the film world to stand briefly with us, acknowledging the apparatus of the narrative that has created this succession of repeating mishaps. And so, as well as conveying exasperation, the look constitutes a moment of understanding between Ollie and the audience: that we each see the way things have played out and will continue to play out, and that we possess a shared appreciation that this is a condition of the structure in place. And of course, the look to camera also marks out a fundamental distinction between Ollie and his audience: we are only observers of his predicament whereas, for him, it is a living experience replete with frustration and, indeed, pain. It might be that we are therefore asked, in light terms, to concede that our entertainment is effectively reliant upon his suffering.

Ollie looks down, wrinkles his nose a little, and shifts his gaze to the left of the frame, out and up towards the spot at which Stan still stands. Stan's response is wordless and wandering as he lightly touches his mouth, turns to follow Ollie's gaze back up the flight of stairs, and then turns back towards his associate as he places a hand on his bow tie. These actions display Stan's characteristic partial obliviousness to events unfolding around him and the concomitant passivity that marks out his behaviour. Indeed, these qualities have contributed to the piano falling once again back to the start (Stan absentmindedly walking away from it to stand with Ollie at the front door) and, as a result, Ollie's gaze back up the steps in Stan's direction identifies and isolates the source of his current predicament. We return to Ollie, seated on the pavement, and he issues one more very slight glance in our direction before shuffling his body around towards Stan and beckoning him wildly with both arms raised above his head, shouting: 'Come here!' The energetic effort throws him off balance and, in contrast, Stan calmly raises his hands tentatively to his hat and begins to plod down the steps. The brief glance offers a small point of punctuation within Ollie's actions, as he transitions from a position of defeat and diminishment on the pavement to seek out a new direction, returning to the job of shifting the piano and enlisting Stan in that endeavour once more. The look to the camera draws the audience into the inevitability of his decision; we each understand he is always bound to return to the repeating cycle and rise and fall, success followed by failure, resolution followed by calamity. Ollie looks at us as if to make sure we understand his place in his world, just as he understands it so completely and fully. It is important that immediately afterward he should look towards Stan because, as well as singling out his partner as the cause of many catastrophes, he also identifies him as an accomplice in the recurring pursuits he now returns to. The beckoning arms and shouted 'Come here!' are emphatic gestures to restart the process and bring Stan back into it. Whilst, no doubt, there is more than a hint of aggression in Ollie's framing of his invite, there is also energy and enthusiasm in the way he not only throws himself back into the game but also resurrects Stan's place within it: at his side. Crucially, whatever tribulations Stan and Ollie face or, indeed, create for themselves, they experience them together. We might say that partnership is crucial to enduring the demands of *The Music Box*'s repetitions and, as a result, Ollie identifies and embraces both the frequent catalyst for chaotic disruption and the source of his survival within it.

These concerns keep us largely within the world of this particular film, as Ollie commits himself to the continuing circularity of its comedic narrative. However, we might broaden this appreciation to consider the ways in which Ollie's behaviour references not only his immediate situation but also the wider film *oeuvre* of Laurel and Hardy. *The Music Box* is particularly reliant upon patterns of repetition as the duo continually try and fail to deliver the piano to the house. But the slapstick routines, the catchphrases, the comic manners, and gestures all find echoes across the whole of their screen appearances. We might say that when Ollie looks at us, acknowledges his position, and then resumes the task of delivering the piano, he is recommitting to a role he performs across all of his films. His self-awareness, therefore, extends beyond this film, stretching out to encompass all of the works that he and Stan have featured in and all of those that they will continue to make after *The Music Box*. In this way, Ollie forges a connection with the audience, with his place within this specific film, and finally with the whole body of Laurel and Hardy films that, taken together, form a cycle of playful recurrences, returns, and repetitions. It makes sense, therefore, that Ollie's look to the camera – his addressing of us – should remain a regular facet across a number of the films in which he and Stan starred. It is as though he reminds us, at certain points, of his place within a broader circular pattern of screen comedy that extends from film to film. And, crucially, his look to the audience is always followed by his return to the comic world, and to his comic companion. The look is tinged with frustration, but that quality never overwhelms him or curtails his actions. Rather, Ollie pauses, accepts the conditions of his screen existence, and returns.

Repetition and Restriction

Whilst the films of Laurel and Hardy can be viewed in relation to each, so potentially revealing those patterns of repetition that Ollie's look to the camera in *The Music Box* seems to acknowledge, they are not sequential instalments of an overarching, continuing narrative. Those kinds of connections are maintained, however, in film sequels and prequels. Stuart Henderson has considered the ways in which sequels can not only provide us with events that are replicated to various degrees from one film to the next but also offer a self-referential awareness of this replication:

> Although the reiteration of a joke or humorous situation can be an end in itself, such references may simultaneously fulfil another, seemingly classical function. In *Die Hard 2* [Renny Harlin 1990], when John McClaine [Bruce Willis] finds himself once again exploring the hidden spaces of a modern building (in this case Washington DC's Dulles airport) in pursuit of terrorists, his response, spoken aloud to no-one in particular, is 'Man I can't fucking believe this: another elevator. How can the same shit happen to the same guy twice?' On the one hand, this comment has no direct narrative purpose, it neither aids nor restricts our construction of the *Die Hard 2* fabula and we might therefore dismiss it as an amusing diversion. On the other, in referring the viewer back to the events of *Die Hard* [John McTiernan 1988], it augments our understanding of McClane as a consistent character: a man who will foolhardily enter into a similar and similarly dangerous situation despite prior experience; a man whose mode of speech, as in the first film, is straightforward and foul-mouthed; and a man who, as in the first film, talks to himself in such intense situations, providing a running commentary on his own actions.
>
> (Henderson 2014, 131–132)

Although we may find cause to query Henderson's claim that McClaine's words have 'no direct narrative purpose' (given that such a reading could risk regarding narrative as involving only the linear processes of plot development), we can extend his points regarding the enrichment of character detail to consider the ways in which McClaine's short speech might also represent the film's attempt to offer allowances for the repetition of a dramatic scenario across *Die Hard* and *Die Hard 2* by making a humorous reference to that recurrence. Moreover, this lighter, comedic tone might also reflect the playfulness and pleasure that can be contained in such repetitions, whereby we might find enjoyment in seeing characters electing or being made to re-tread familiar paths (even when they are less enamoured with this fate).

Henderson's example from *Die Hard 2* demonstrates one way in which repetition can become a point of reference (and, indeed, self-reference), the impact of which is achieved through brevity and lightness: the delivery of short lines that establish a shared acknowledgement between the audience and the film that certain repeated structures are in play. Elsewhere in franchise cinema, repetition can become a more sustained element and even a fundamental structuring feature. *Avengers: Endgame* (Anthony Russo/Joe Russo 2019), for example, marks the culmination of a series of storylines that had effectively been developing, to greater and lesser extents, across eleven years and twenty-one previous film releases within the 'Marvel Cinematic Universe.' A large portion of *Endgame*'s plot, however, is devoted to its central ensemble of characters travelling back in time to revisit events, characters, and locations from those preceding films. This could be regarded as a device to, for example, reinforce the scale of a wider narrative that stretches across all of those earlier films and all of those years, or to reward audience investment in them, or even by this stage to offer a nostalgic return to the past for fans of the series. All of which may be true, but is also the case that this re-treading of footsteps already imprinted is an embedded element within the narrative that possesses a logical purpose as the group of heroes travel into the past in order to retrieve a set of 'Infinity Stones' that will reverse the catastrophic event of half the universe's inhabitant being obliterated. As a consequence, the journey backward moves events forward and, in addition, provides some opportunities to strengthen and deepen character portrayals as they encounter the strains and complications of their time-travelling quests. In this respect, we might at least begin to suggest that this onscreen resurrection of a familiar past contains degrees of purpose and momentum within the series' fictional storytelling.

We can consider this form of repetition against another franchise, the 'Star Wars' films, and *The Rise of Skywalker* (J.J. Abrams 2019), which was released in the same year as *Endgame*. *The Rise of Skywalker* (hereafter *Rise*) forms part of the 'Skywalker Saga,' which had already amassed eight films, divided into three sets of trilogies across forty years (with *Rise* belonging to the last of these). By the time of *Rise*'s release, the 'saga' had already become characterised strongly by patterns of repetition. It is perhaps tempting to see the prequel trilogy as the most prominent catalyst for this, containing as it does a great abundance of visual compositions, plot points, musical motifs, and character dialogue that reference directly or even replicate moments from the original trilogy. Such a perception might be supported by the now-infamous observations from director (and 'Star Wars' creator) George Lucas that Anakin Skywalker's destruction of a ship that controls an army of robots in the first film of the prequel trilogy, *The Phantom Menace* (George Lucas 1999) is a direct equivalent of Luke Skywalker's destruction of the 'Death Star' in the first film of the original trilogy, *A New Hope* (George Lucas 1977). Lucas mentions that 'It's like poetry, sort of: they rhyme. Every stanza kind of rhymes with the last one. Hopefully, it'll work …' Lucas' words arguably constitute a particular understanding of what 'rhyme' can be in poetry: that it relates literally to the last word of each line rhyming with another. There is nothing inherently wrong with this perception, of course, but it does suggest a somewhat straightforward approach that might limit the potential for subtle evocation or delicate echoing across films and, as a consequence, could become a constraining structure for expression. Certainly, the 'rhyming' in the prequel trilogy is notably blunt but, in truth, this pattern had already been established in the original trilogy.[3] This ranges from the relatively playful repetition of lines such as 'I have a bad feeling about this' (which recurs even within *A New Hope*), to the mirrored resemblance of events like Darth Vader cutting off Luke Skywalker's hand in *The Empire Strikes Back* (Irvin Kershner 1980) and Luke then cutting off Vader's hand in *The Return of the Jedi* (Richard Marquand 1983). And, pertinent to Lucas' quotation, *Return of the Jedi* features a second 'Death Star,' which will be destroyed again, the band of Rebels having received vital schematic plans of the space station from a unit of brave spies, mirroring precisely the events of *A New Hope*. Indeed, the structure of *The Return of the Jedi* provides a close copy of *A New Hope* to some extent, with the first section of the film devoted to a rescue mission (Han Solo in the later film, Princess Leia in the earlier work) before the co-ordinated assault on the 'Death Star.' However, it is another character, Lando Calrissian, who ultimately fires the shot that destroys the second 'Death Star' and not a Skywalker at all, which at least disrupts the line of poetic continuity that Lucas hopes to construct in the mirrored events of *New Hope* and *Phantom Menace*. It appears to be more the case that any character can be drawn into the films' repeating patterns, and that their selection is often somewhat indiscriminate rather than forming part of an overarching, coherent plan.

Why should the 'Star Wars' series fall into patterns of repetition relatively quickly? On the one hand, it may simply reveal Lucas' preference for these kinds of structures, perhaps conforming to a notion that universal events are somehow connected by mysterious resonances (just as the 'Force' is depicted as a kind of widespread binding element in these films). Equally, however, we might note that one significant achievement of the first three 'Star Wars' films is their inherent and endearing simplicity. Characters are imbued with essentially straightforward and uncomplicated motivations: primarily the various Rebel forces fighting for 'good' against the 'evil' of the Empire. Even when characters apparently change course, they are guided by relatively traditional and simple impulses of love: a previously mercenary Han Solo chooses to fight with the Rebellion due to his burgeoning union with Luke and Leia; a previously duplicitous Lando helps the Rebels due to an enduring friendship with Han Solo; and even Darth Vader – a potentially conflicted character – rejects the evil Empire and kills the Emperor because he loves his son, Luke (thus reciprocating the faithful devotion that Luke shows for him). This results in an array of characterisations that are strongly defined but, at the same time, are not required to be complex and therefore possess relatively little depth. It is perhaps inevitable, then, that drawing this shallow source material out across three and then six and, finally, nine films could place an emphasis upon repeating events and motifs rather than leading to the development of richer and more intricate portraits of its characters. The prequel trilogy devotes itself to telling the story of Anakin Skywalker's moral descent from heroic young Jedi to evil Sith lord. Yet, a short and mournful description of this conversion, provided by Obi Wan Kenobi in *Return of the Jedi*, is arguably more compelling and impactful than the following extensive depiction, due precisely to its brevity and its ambiguity. The 'Star Wars' films (and by implication, Lucas) do not appear well-equipped to explore dark tragedy and so, at least initially, this painful transition is placed appropriately both in the past and off-screen until the decision is taken to depict it at greater length.

The first film of the sequel trilogy, *The Force Awakens* (J.J. Abrams 2015), returns to a familiar pattern as its story culminates in the destruction of yet another Empire-built 'Death Star' by a group of Rebel fighters. Similarly, *Rise* copies overtly the repetitions of the original trilogy by again featuring the climactic obliteration of, essentially, a rebuilt 'Death Star' equivalent (now a whole array of planet-destroying weapons mounted on countless huge spaceships), just as *Return of the Jedi* emulated the conclusion of *A New Hope*. Indeed, by this stage, *Rise* is mirroring closely *Return of the Jedi*'s finale, with a magically-resurrected Emperor attempting to persuade a young Jedi (Rey now in place of Luke) to join him, with the latter resisting and subsequently finding assistance from a former leader of the Empire (Kylo Ren now substituting for Darth Vader).

With victory secured, an epilogue sequence continues this pattern of revisitations yet further. Rey flies to the planet Tatooine, passing over a Jawa transport vehicle first seen in *A New Hope*. Having landed, she walks towards the Lar homestead, where Luke Skywalker was raised, providing another familiar sight from *A New Hope*. Arriving at the site, she finds a piece of scrap metal and slides down a sloping sand embankment, replicating her previous actions from *The Force Awakens* (with John Williams' score now incorporating Rey's theme from the earlier film on the soundtrack as she descends). She looks around this space, as though reflecting upon its ambient history and then we cut to a series of close-up shots as Rey places two lightsabres, Luke's and Leia's, on a cloth and carefully wraps them up, ties the package and places her hand gently upon it. We cut again to Rey outside the homestead, kneeling, with the package positioned before her on the sand. We zoom in as the music swells and the lightsabre package sinks down into the sand under the influence of Rey's telekinetic 'Force' powers. She ignites her own lightsabre but rapidly lowers it when an inquisitive passing woman asks who she is. Rey introduces herself by her first name, to which the woman enquires further: 'Rey who?' Rey looks out across the horizon, John Williams' familiar 'Force' theme emerges on the soundtrack and the ghost visions of both Luke and Leia materialise gradually. We zoom in to a close-up of Rey as she acknowledges their presence, then to a reverse shot of the ghosts more vivid and distinct, before returning to Rey as she finishes her introduction: 'Rey Skywalker.' The musical 'Force' theme carries over to new shots depicting Rey and her robot companion, BB8, walking in front of twin setting suns, stopping to look out at the scene, their forms framed and silhouetted against the two circles of light. This image replicates directly a moment from *A New Hope* in which Luke also stares out at the sunsets, from almost the same spot, thus establishing a further and final visual resemblance within the scene.

Figure 1.4 The Rise of Skywalker.

Figure 1.5 Star Wars: A New Hope.

This final sequence is emphatic in its accumulation of references and repetitions. In terms of this fictional world's integral logic, at least, we might note at least some curious choices: Rey decides to bury the lightsabres at a site which hold almost no significance for Leia, where Luke's family were brutally murdered and from which he longed to escape in his youth (indeed, the scene that Rey replicates, in which he stares out at the sunsets, is surely representative of his yearning for a life beyond the horizon of farm work on Tatooine). It seems at least questionable that either of the siblings would have regarded it with particular fondness, and thus as an appropriate resting place for treasured belongings. However, Tatooine and this home are familiar and perhaps iconic locations for audiences of these films, and so the choice of setting appears to depend upon viewers' recollection or even nostalgic remembrance, rather than following any firm character motivation. Leaving those considerations aside, it seems ironically appropriate that Rey should submerge the weapons in a layer of sand, as though symbolising the fundamental impermanence of any apparent resolution in this fictional universe. These lightsabres can be retrieved in the future, just as seemingly any scene, storyline or character can be recreated, revisited or resurrected in the 'Star Wars' series of films. As this process repeats again and again, meaning and significance arguably become diminished further and further, with every conclusion ostensibly reversible and any new scenario potentially functioning as an echo of past events. In this way, repetition not only features as a fundamental structuring element in the 'Star Wars' series, but it also becomes a trap of sorts that each film must negotiate or fall into.[4] *Rise*'s epilogue scene seems to encapsulate this dilemma, as the repeating of motifs and actions becomes a central element, yet this repetition possesses sparse internal logic or coherent dramatic purpose. We might, therefore, consider the inherent structure of the 'Star Wars' series results ultimately in a form of repetition for repetition's sake only, placing creative constraints upon opportunities for expression, meaning, and significance within the films.

To conclude, in this chapter I have attempted to outline some notions of repetition and the ways in which they might relate to specific examples, moving through the visual (*Tetris*), audio (Pachelbel's Canon), and audio-visual (*The Music Box* and *Rise of Skywalker*). As a way of opening up sets of ideas and incorporating a consideration of moments from particular texts, the discussion of each text has been kept necessarily brief, and it is certainly the case that particular lines of enquiry could be pursued further, just as notions of repetition can no doubt be applied to a much greater range of case studies from video games, musical compositions, and films. However, attending to these other media, even in relatively sparse terms, provides a basis for moving the discussion on to this book's primary interest: the relationships between television and repetition. Whilst it would be inaccurate to suggest that different art forms represent any themes or interests in the same way (and, indeed, the representation of themes and interests of art forms can vary significantly within individual art forms themselves), it is nevertheless useful to think across disciplinary boundaries, especially in relation to a theme as broad and wide-ranging as repetition. Within this chapter, it has been useful to consider video games, music, and film as a means of visiting certain concepts relating to notions of repetition and, whilst we should acknowledge that these may change form or shape in the study of television, it has been advantageous to open space across different media to advance preliminary observations. Although I would endeavour to suggest that television provides some potent and engaging configurations of repetition, I am not, in proceeding to make it a main focus of study, suggesting that it possesses a special relationship to the theme that, implicitly, these other art forms do not. Indeed, I would contend that any of them would make equally appropriate case studies, and encourage that work.

I hope that it has become equally apparent, throughout the pages of this opening chapter, that I am not committing myself to an exacting version of repetition and that, in attending to the work of writers like Kawin, Bellour, and Eco, I am drawn to their common assertion that notions of repetition are often, and necessarily, imprecise, relying often upon a *sense* of repetition and rarely, if ever, insisting upon absolute precision. That lack of exactitude might otherwise be undesirable in the study of any thematic interest but, here, we might instead note that this kind of ambiguity more accurately reflects not only the ways in which repetition is evoked in works of art but also our human experience of it. On those grounds, we may regard it as a practical basis from which to proceed.

Notes

1 Although there are many variations available, and the format does not vary too radically, I should note that the version of *Tetris* I am referring to in my description is from the Nintendo Entertainment System, played through emulation software on an Apple Macintosh computer.

2 Examples of songs incorporating Pachelbel's Canon include The Farm's *All Together Now* (1990), The Pet Shop Boys' *Go West* (1993), Coolio (featuring 40 Thevz)'s *C U When U Get There* (1997), Vitamin C's *Graduation (Friends Forever)* (2000) and Maroon 5's *Memories* (2019).

3 This perhaps offers a rather negative perception of the prequel trilogy and, indeed, the 'Star Wars' saga in general. With this in mind, I should mention that a very positive appraisal of Lucas' work can be

found in Camille Paglia's lively account of the third film in the prequel trilogy, *The Revenge of the Sith* (George Lucas, 2005). Paglia contends that Lucas possesses 'one of the most powerful and tenacious minds in contemporary culture' (Paglia, 2013: 190), and is entirely complementary of *Revenge*, stating, for example, that 'The exhilarating eight-minute battle over Coruscant that opens *Revenge of the Sith*, with its dense cloud of stately destroyers, swooping starfighters, and fiendish buzz droids, cuts optical pathways that are as graceful and abstract as the weightless skeins in a drip painting by Jackson Pollock (Ibid: 185). Paglia also expresses a positive regard for one aspect of repetition in the Star Wars films, observing that: '*Star Wars* takes a cyclical view of history, seeing democracy defeated again and again by fascism and imperialism, from Caesar to Napoleon and Hitler' (Ibid: 187).

4 In this respect, it is worth reflecting on the second film in the final 'saga' trilogy, *The Last Jedi* (Rian Johnson 2017). This instalment is notorious for resisting certain preconceived expectations that audiences may have held regarding the parameters for likely events within this fictional universe and, indeed, the behaviour of some of the film's central characters. So, for example, Luke Skywalker is initially presented as a somewhat disillusioned figure, possessing no reverence for the 'Force' and little interest in becoming a mentor for Rey. This portrayal reverses a set of characteristics that had been developed in the original trilogy and, as a consequence, might suggest that Johnson's contribution escapes fairly dramatically the 'trap' of repetition that other films arguably fall into. Yet, the reversal of Luke's characteristic traits is ultimately revealed to be a precursor to his redemption and restoration as a hero of the 'Force.' Furthermore, however radical the changes that Johnson made to the series were, they are all effectively erased in the next film, *Rise*, which instead provides an extremely close rendition of plot structures from previous films. Therefore, any evasion of the repetition 'trap' is partial and short-lived when the series is viewed as a whole, with a return to familiar ground re-established with relative speed and ease. Finally, any new direction that Johnson attempts to plot can be seen as a reaction against the previously-established structures of repetition and, so, are effectively judged against those preceding iterations. As a result, a vocal fan community enthusiastically registered its displeasure at a formula being disrupted, revealing that repetition can entrench expectations and that it is actually quite difficult to successfully negotiate a move away from them. Consequently, the trap of repetition is still a significant pressure, and one that appears hard to evade.

2   Television and Repetition

Having explored in relatively brief terms some aspects of repetition in other forms, we can turn our attention to this book's main interest: the relationship between television and repetition. Although repetition may not have been a strong guiding focus in television studies, the theme has nevertheless emerged and shaped certain approaches and ideas within the discipline. It is worth beginning with this work, I would suggest, as a means of marking out a basis for a consideration of repetition in particular television texts. This is not to suggest its centrality to the study of television, as though repetition were some spectral influence whose pivotal importance was always there and is somehow made visible if we only look at it directly, but instead to regard it as one element that interweaves with certain debates and the development of conceptual understandings. From there, we can begin to hone our interests in repetition and focus more closely on texts possessing potent connections with the theme, to the extent that it becomes a key facet in their aesthetic and narrative structuring.

Forms of Repetition in Television

A range of scholars and commentators have illustrated the ways in which television possesses inherent qualities that are aligned with the concept of repetition, as well as corresponding with generalised notions and experiences of repetition. The various configurations of this relationship are multifarious and wide-ranging, positioned at differing levels of directness, with different works placing the weight of emphasis in a variety of ways. Roger Silverstone's influential study, *Television and Everyday Life*, for example, explores television's relationship to the routines and rituals of domestic and public life in depth and detail. In the opening pages of his work, he considers the forms and characteristics of ontological security as a fundamental aspect of everyday life, and television's relationship to it. He proposes that:

> Ontological security is sustained through the familiar and the predictable. Our commonsense attitudes and beliefs express and sustain our

DOI: 10.4324/9781003265283-3

practical understandings of the world, without which life would quickly become intolerable. Common sense is sustained by practical knowledge and expressed and supported by a whole range of symbols and symbolic formations. The symbols of daily life: the everyday sights and sounds of natural language and familiar culture; the publicly broadcast media texts on billboards, in newspapers, on television; the highly charged and intense private and public rituals in domestic or national rites of passage or international celebrations; all these symbols, in their continuity, their drama and their ambiguity, are also bids for control.

(Silverstone 1994, 19)

Although the term 'repetition' is not made overt in this account, it is not difficult to see how it might relate to the 'familiar and predictable' elements of 'daily life,' which possess the essential quality of recurring precisely through being 'daily' and therefore become 'familiar and predictable' through their cycles of repetition. Silverstone's important assertion, however, is that the assembly of symbols within daily life contributes to attitudes and beliefs (somewhat ambiguously described as 'common sense') that provide a sense of ontological security – that make life bearable. It is a potent notion and one that provides Silverstone's arguments with a foundation that might be seen to have a relationship to questions more regularly associated with forms of existential debate. At the least, he asserts in relatively strong terms that familiarity and predictability within daily life is crucial to maintaining a balanced and rational sense *of* that daily life (which I take the term 'common sense' to be an allusion to). Placing television within that system of routines, rituals, and symbols, therefore, has significant implications for the ways in which we evaluate the position and purpose of that medium within the wider ontological experience. Silverstone introduces television in the following way:

What is the issue here? It is the place of television in the visible and hidden ordering of everyday life; in its spatial and temporal significance; in its embeddedness in quotidian patterns and habits, as a contributor to our security. Television as object: the screen providing the focus of our daily rituals and the frame for the limited transcendence – the suspension of disbelief – which marks our excursions from the profane routines of the daily grind into the sacred routines of schedules and programmes.

(Ibid, 19)[1]

Importantly, here, Silverstone outlines television's fundamental integration within the 'patterns and habits' of everyday life and, as a consequence, positions it as crucial to any sense we might possess of the ontological security he mentions earlier. Moving to a consideration of 'television as object,' he regards a key attribute of the medium to be its capacity for offering the opportunity to 'transcend' the routines of daily life and, indeed, replace them with the routines of 'schedules and programmes' (in the 1994 world his book was published in). This notion of the viewer escaping real life in some way through the act of watching television (or, for that matter, many other forms of media) was hardly new at the time of Silverstone's writing and might be viewed as a branch of the traditional 'uses and gratifications' theory with an emphasis on the viewer's dependency upon media forms. It is a curious perspective for Silverstone to adopt, however, given that he also appears to be arguing that television is profoundly amalgamated with the rhythms of daily life, rather than enjoying a position of transcendence – however limited – over those rituals and routines. Nevertheless, whether we take the view that television represents an excursion from the 'profane routines of the daily grind,' and to what extent, Silverstone's account certainly conveys a sense of this activity being undertaken regularly and, indeed, repetitively, precisely because he describes television being turned to, for whatever reason, within a daily cycle of everyday existence. Although viewing habits have undoubtedly changed since the publication of Silverstone's book, with the prominence of scheduling as a structuring influence diminished in an era of streaming that has ushered in self-scheduling as a result of increased accessibility, it is nevertheless the case that television viewing remains closely entwined to the cyclical rhythms of daily life in the ways that he describes. The nature of that relationship is based fundamentally upon repetition because everyday existence is itself defined by patterns of repetitive behaviour (even if we are just as likely to be watching shows via mobile devices on the daily commute rather than that engagement being necessarily restricted only to the domestic setting, for example).

In relation to this theme, John Ellis' equally influential work on segmentation in television takes into account the idea that repetition is an aspect of the medium at a fundamental level. Ellis is pursuing a somewhat closer focus on aspects of television content in relation to repetition, whereas Silverstone arguably brings his emphasis into contact with broader sociological concerns, and he sets out his argument in the following way:

> The segment form implies repetition: TV's characteristic form of repetition is the series or the serial, a form of continuity-with-difference that TV has perfected. This form fosters the segmental approach, the generation of large numbers of diverse coherent and relatively self-contained elements. The serial implies a certain narrative progression and a conclusion; the series does not: whether

documentary, drama or everlasting soap opera, it has no end in view. The series always envisages its own return. The series itself divides into two types: fictional series that are centred around a particular situation and set of characters, and non-fictional series that are characterised by a recurring format and known set of routines.

(Ellis 1997 [1982], 122–123)

Within his concept of the segmental in television, Ellis identifies the series and serial as the forms that best characterise aspects of repetition to slightly differing extents. Indeed, he seems to regard the series as displaying characteristic recurrence and open-endedness, with 'no end in view' as it repeatedly 'envisages its own return.' In his account, Ellis works in relatively broad terms as he lays out some distinctions in his choice of examples, to support his arguments so that 'series' can extend to documentary, drama or 'everlasting' soap opera, and in his suggestion that fictional series are 'centred around a particular situation and set of characters' whereas non-fictional series are 'characterised by a recurring format and known set of routines.' In one sense, it would be useful to consider the first set of points in a little more detail in order, for example, to tease out some of the distinctions that also exist between the documentary, drama, and soap opera formats (and consequently, with our interests in mind, how they each create a convey a sense of not only neverendingness but also repetition), and, equally, whether there exists an essential cross-fertilisation between the categories of fiction and non-fiction as Ellis describes them. It seems possible, for instance, that a non-fictional show might be centred around a particular situation and set of characters (even if those 'characters' are non-actors within a documentary setting) or that a fictional show might incorporate a recurring format and known set of routines. In making tentative suggestions of this kind, it is perhaps worth considering the historical context in which Ellis' work was first disseminated, and whether the boundaries between fiction and non-fiction were more firmly defined in the ways that he suggests, and before the advent of, for example, scripted reality television shows, which certainly display characteristics more commonly associated with fictional drama (indeed, centred around a particular situation and a set of 'characters').

Nevertheless, as I have already suggested, Ellis' arguments do rely upon a closer consideration of the actual content of television, rather than considering its function as a mechanical device that exists in the realm of everyday routines (in some senses, not unlike ovens that cook the daily meal or washing machines that regularly clean clothes, so becoming integrated into the rhythms and structures of domestic life) in the way that Silverstone might allude to. Ellis' work joins with Silverstone's, however, in positioning repetition as a fundamental characteristic of television, both in terms of its content and the ways in which we experience it. Derek Kompare's study of 'Rerun TV' extends this focus as he seeks to underline television's fundamental and long-standing relationship with repeat content. He provides an initial context for this position in the following way:

> Whether originally produced for theatrical release or made for television, extant films and videotapes have always dominated American television. Even during the 1920s and 1930s, when commercial television was only speculative, experimental broadcasters relied more on existing films than they did on live performances. In the late 1940s, old films from Hollywood and Britain regularly appeared on the new medium. Within a few years, filmed programs that had been made for television were beginning to be repeated. As television became a dominant national institution in the 1950s and 1960s, these repeats became standard programming fare on every station, continually presenting and representing "the past" as an interminable array of feature films, short subjects, cartoons, newsreel clips, and cancelled network series. During the 1970s and 1980s, this repetition became tacitly acknowledged as an historical source, helping foster the national memory of television via the construction of a "television heritage." Since that point, reruns have become one of the primary products of television, fueling unprecedented industrial synergies and corporate branding, while becoming ensconced in American popular culture, and fostering experiences and practices of television structured around continual repetition.
>
> (Kompare 2005, x–xi)

It is worth noting that Kompare is writing about the US television context (and indeed, his book is titled *Rerun Nation*), which should at least remind us that 'television' is not necessarily a universal term that possesses the same cultural and historical meanings across territories. A valuable aspect of his account, however, lies in his clear laying out of the ways in which the showing of repeat material was an inherent feature of television at even an early stage of its development as a medium, rather than something that emerges gradually over a period of its development (due to factors such as the generation of material that *can* be repeated or the expansion of available channels that, straightforwardly, provides increased screen time needing to be filled with, we might presume, relatively inexpensive content). Nevertheless, Kompare is careful to acknowledge that, in the passage of time, the repeating of content has at least grown in prevalence, leading to the situation that he describes whereby reruns become 'one of the primary products of television' and 'experiences and practices of television' are 'structured around continuous repetition.' These observations, taken on their own merits, not only provide a useful basis for under-standing a key characteristic of the television landscape but also, as a result, establish a firm foundation for Kompare's wider study of reruns specifically. However, he expands upon such assertions to provide further motivation for pursuing this focus and, consequently, offers another guiding influence for the concentration upon content repetition in televi-sion. He notes that:

> Despite this overwhelming repetition, television's ontology, its "es-sence," is still said to reside in its "liveness": its ability to transmit events as they happen to millions of receivers across the nation or even world ... However, what if this liveness assumption is wrong? What if television is not the ideal conduit for "live," news events, but is instead a machine of repetition, geared toward the constant circulation of recorded, already-seen events?
>
> (Kompare 2005, xi)

Although Kompare does not provide an indication of the ways in which an emphasis upon television's 'liveness' is articulated and, indeed, by whom, we would not struggle to recognise that, even broadly, the immediacy and simultaneity of the medium has been recognised as a central ontological trait, and one that distinguishes it, for example, from other comparable mediums such as cinema which, for fairly obvious and understandable reasons, is seen to occur in the past tense whereas, in contrast, television possesses the potential to function in the present tense. Take, for example, John Ellis' influential, guiding assertion that the twentieth century is a century of 'witness,' and the powerful con-tribution television, alongside other visual, audio, and audio-visual media, has made to that process:

> Photographic images bring us into the position of witness because they are mechanical reproductions. They have a relative inability to discriminate between subject and setting. Above all, they strike us with their haunting sense of being the death-mask imprint of a moment that is already past (if on film) or fleeting and almost ungraspable (if on live television).
>
> (Ellis 2000, 10)

Statements of this kind provide, we might contend, an accurate account of the ways in which events may be captured and understood in com-plementary but differing ways according to whether they appear osten-sibly to belong in the past tense '(on film)' or in the present '(on live television).' Kompare's argument, however, is that this should not constitute the dominant way in which we discriminate between mediums and, furthermore, perceive television. His central contention is that, when the actual content of television programming is regarded more fully and in detail, a picture emerges instead of television being characterised at least as strongly (and, in Kompare's view, *more* prominently) as a medium comprised of 'past tense' material as a result of the abundance of repeated material that is shown regularly, which has the potential to make the point of divergence from film content less clearly or securely defined. Hence his potent description of television as a 'machine of repetition.'

One issue might be that, even if we accept Kompare's points about television being as much about 'the constant circulation of recorded, already-seen events' as live, immediate occurrences, the very notion of repetition on television carries with it certain negative associations, perceptions, and judgements. Broadly speaking, we may recognise a vocalised sense that an abundance of repeated content on television is an undesirable and unwelcome quality. A cursory look at stories from various newspapers provides numerous examples of this attitude, with headlines such as 'BBC boss sparks outrage after claiming viewers "love repeats" at Christmas – as it emerges over two-thirds of festive content BBC 1 and 2 has been aired before' (Ardehali 2018) constituting a somewhat typical illustration from the UK press. Although the accompanying story contains only tenuous suggestions of a genuine 'outrage,' with the closest version being a quotation from a government minister that the profusion of repeats is 'disappointing,' the headline from the *Daily Mail* nevertheless captures the sense that repetition of content on television is worthy of comment and, furthermore, might be regarded as unsatisfactory.[2] Hence, we are presented with a somewhat manufactured 'outrage' at such an occurrence, even at a time of year when viewers might be expected to tolerate repeats a little more charitably due to feelings of possible nostalgia and a connection with broadcasting history being attached to festive programming of the past.

Such attitudes are not restricted only to the mainstream media, however. Raymond Williams' landmark 1974 contribution to the study of television, *Television: Technology and Cultural Form*, for example, contains the following observation regarding the then-emerging technology of cable television within the United States:

> The irony is that the best-financed cable companies are offering what is, essentially, a version of the very worst kind of broadcasting service. It is not uncommon for a twelve-channel cable system to be planned to carry nothing but old movies or old television entertainment series. The choice which is offered as a fruit of the new technology is a choice only within this repetitive dimension.
>
> (Williams [1974] 2003, 145)

Williams' account is notable for setting out a very clearly articulated viewpoint regarding the prospect of heavily repeated content on television: that it would represent 'the very worst kind of broadcasting service' and that, although cable television brings with it a wider range of channels, and therefore choice, any choice exists 'only within this repetitive dimension.' It is not difficult to ascertain that, for Williams, repetition is unequivocally a bad thing for television, and that little or no value can be found in a channel or group of channels being devoted only to the broadcasting of repeated content. And yet, as Kompare argues, such an abundance of repeats is not novel in television and, if we follow his line of reasoning, contributes to television's essential status as a 'machine of repetition.' Nevertheless, we might find that Williams' perspective is not uncommon to us and, furthermore, not only are we familiar with it but might share in the perception that repeats are somehow a less attractive feature of television content.

The assorted accounts of repetition in television mentioned thus far each possesses the shared characteristic of discussing the medium at a relative distance from the observable content on screen: the shows themselves. This does not necessarily represent an issue and, indeed, is consistent with not only the positions that they each set out but also the important contributions they seek to make through their respective scholarship. These writers are, to various degrees, mapping out understandings of television as a medium, rather than focussing on individual television shows. As a consequence, a precise appreciation of how themes of repetition are integrated and expressed within the texts themselves, for example, does not constitute a primary concern within their academic standpoints. That is not to say that *no* work on themes of repetition in television pays attention to content. Indeed, two edited collections that concentrate upon different forms of television remakes, *American Remakes of British Television: Transformations and Mistranslations* (Lavigne and Marcovitch 2011) and *Remake Television: Reboot, Re-use, Recycle* (Lavigne 2014), are organised into chapters whereby separate contributors, by and large, base arguments around a specific television text or texts that have been 'remade,' either within or across national contexts, according to the respective interests of the two books. Undoubtedly, such an approach brings us closer to a consideration of television content than the studies mentioned thus far, as shows become a structuring element in the various chapters to varying extents. However, it is also the case that individual shows are discussed as illustrative elements of a broader process of repetition – the remake – in television. As a consequence, there tends to be sparse attention paid to the ways in which repetition is approached, handled, and expressed as a thematic concern *within* these shows. In this respect, it might be said that we are moving only a very short distance from the kinds of discussion found in the work of Silverstone, Ellis, Kompare, and Williams.

Television Revisiting Television

Again, this absence of a sustained focus on shows' creative utilisation of repetition is not necessarily something that should be troubling, indicating as it does the pursual of directions that aim, ostensibly, to provide a picture of specific trends in television (the idea of national and transnational remakes, for example). However, it is equally the case that merits can be found in the appreciation of repetition as a feature within individual shows. And, here, we might turn to a case like the long-running title *Gogglebox* (Channel 4, 2013-), which was first aired in the UK on Channel 4 and has since led to a number of international adaptations, as well as spinoff shows such as *Gogglesprogs* (featuring children), *Celebrity Gogglebox* (featuring celebrities) and *Vlogglebox* (with teens and young adults watching online content). The premise of the show is that, in their various domestic living room settings, family or friendship groups watch a selection of programmes which aired that week and talk about them (around and amongst conversations about their own lives). Their viewing reactions are then filmed and intercut in the show's edit with corresponding clips from those shows. A large amount of the onscreen content, therefore, consists of material that has already appeared on television – a collection of shows that have already aired – with the only 'original' content being the reactions of the family or friendship groups as they watch. As a consequence, there is at least a chance (sometimes even a likelihood) that viewers of *Gogglebox* will be watching sections of shows they have already seen. Indeed, the linking voiceover (provided by Craig Cash and, previously, by Caroline Aherne[3]) encourages the audience to feel part of a repeated viewing experience, regularly using phrases like 'this week, *we* were watching ...' [my italics] and 'many of *us* watched ...' [my italics] in their scripted narration. Clearly, the format of *Gogglebox* involves an integrated employment of repetition as a central structuring element and, indeed, makes a virtue of repeating content, which contrasts with the kind of adverse reactions found in publications such as the *Daily Mail* and in academic accounts provided by Williams. The prominence of repetition within *Gogglebox* is extended further as its seasons accumulate (up to nineteen by 2022) and the same basic format is recapitulated over and over again. Furthermore, although there is a gradual turnover of family and friendship groups over time, it is generally the same non-professional cast that we encounter each week, which again contributes to notions of a repeated viewing experience. Additionally, the pieces of music used in the titles and between sequences remain largely unchanged over time, further securing this sense of recurrence. In these ways, we might speculate that there are layers of repetition running through the form and content of *Gogglebox* and that, as a consequence, it represents a crucial facet of our viewing experience.

With such observations in place, however, it is important to consider what the purpose and meaning of repetition in *Gogglebox* might be. Having established the prominence of repeats and repeating structures within the show, we can begin to reflect upon its potential significance. One starting point for this kind of enquiry might be to attend to moments that possess very distinct repetitive qualities and, particularly, moments that recall television events which a viewing audience is more likely to have either seen already or have good prior knowledge of. On Monday 19 September 2022, the funeral of Queen Elizabeth II was watched by a peak national UK audience of an estimated 37.5 million people, and an estimated global audience of 4 billion (Molina-Whyte 2022). The event was included in a *Gogglebox* episode broadcast on the Friday of that week, and Cash's voiceover narration mentioned the funeral's large television audience, opening the segment on the event with the words: 'On Monday, over 37 million of us gathered to say farewell to Her Majesty.' This description is not entirely accurate, as that figure of 37.5 million includes viewers who watched for only three minutes or more, which may include very casual viewers rather than everyone necessarily 'gathering' in those numbers to watch the entire service. Nevertheless, the viewing figures are significantly high, representing a substantial television audience, and Cash's voiceover begins to embed an idea of a nation 'coming together,' which will be continued as the sequence progresses. As well as establishing themes of scale and unity, the introduction to this sequence also establishes the tone, as it begins not with the usual, upbeat, incidental music, but instead with the more sombre and slower musical accompaniment taken from the funeral itself. The accompanying shots correspond with the 'gathering' alluded to in the voiceover, as we see the various groupings of *Gogglebox* regulars arriving with drinks, and boxes of tissues, and sitting down to switch on their televisions.

From here, the show strikes a shifting balance from the grand reverence generated by the ceremony itself, and continued in some of the groups' reflections and emotional responses, against the more mundane, lower-key, and even comedic comments they also offer. So, for example, Stephen begins by saying: 'This is how I want my funeral to be … I want the whole of London to come to a standstill,' to which his partner Daniel replies: 'You'll be lucky if you get three people.' In one sense, Stephen's words respond to the impressive tribute to the Queen that has been constructed and the central position she occupied in British life but, at the same time, his tongue-in-cheek self-aggrandisement underscores his words with an intentionally comedic tone, which Daniel responds to as he delivers the deflating punchline to the set-up. This pattern is continued throughout the sequence: a visibly-moved Jenny remarks about the assembled congregation in Westminster Abbey that 'These people have been in there since half-past eight this morning' and her friend Lee follows up with 'I know. [Pause] What if you wanted to go to the toilet? Where would you go?' Jenny replies: 'I think there is a toilet, I think.'

Figure 2.1 Gogglebox.

The exchange captures both an acknowledgement of the apparently impressive dedication the members of the waiting congregation have shown and a meditation upon more everyday, even banal matters. Again, we might note that it possesses a comedic structure as the former is swiftly undercut by the latter. These kinds of structures persist until the very end. The ceremony closes with the Royal bagpiper playing and walking away from the camera before disappearing from view. All of the groups seem captivated by the potential poignancy that this scene creates. Alison, alive to the scene's poetic intentions, says that '... It's how its fading into the background' but (after we have cut back to the piper and then returned to the family group) her daughter Helena observes: 'It's taking a while, int' it? Really. It's taking a bit of a while, this.' Despite how this might scan in written form, Helena's comment isn't pointedly disrespectful: she remains watching the screen, fidgeting only very minimally and, although her words are funny, she doesn't look to her parents for recognition of any comedic intent or to illicit further interaction. Indeed, when the piper finally disappears, she says 'He's gone' with a form of quiet introspection.

Helena's words, in fact, might be seen to encapsulate a point that the whole sequence in *Gogglebox* has been alluding to through the attitudes and behaviours of its cast: that mourning can involve complicated responses and can incorporate the comedic and mundane alongside the reverent and the respectful. *Gogglebox* doesn't do anything so pious as to permit such responses and, instead, might be seen to reassure implicitly that all kinds of reactions are legitimate and are not necessarily oppositional or contradictory. Hence, the individuals in the viewing groups

Figure 2.2 Gogglebox.

fluctuate between different states. In this respect, the show might be seen to encourage the perception that it provides a less mediated, perhaps even more 'authentic,' response to the event than the standard or official commentary of news and current affairs programming.

Returning to the central theme of repetition in relation to a show like *Gogglebox*, there are a number of ways that the revisiting of events from the Queen's funeral might be regarded. It can be seen as contrived for entertainment, for example, by exploring fresh and lively perspectives on the familiar, or as a reinforcement of the notion that we somehow collectively shared in a culturally significant moment, or that returning to the moment provides a platform for displaying and exploring a cross-section of societal attitudes and responses across various classes, age groups, genders, and ethnicities. The exercise could conceivably be regarded as pointlessly repetitive, of course, given that it is very unlikely that the *Gogglebox* audience will not have already seen the funeral, watched clips from it, or engaged with news coverage about it, if we take the estimated viewing figures as a guide. In aiming to resist that charge of pointlessness, I want to reflect upon *Gogglebox*'s repetition in the context of John Ellis' concept of 'working through,' which he discusses in the context of a late-twentieth century television environment. The term derives from Freudian psychoanalysis, whereby 'The subject of the analysis has undergone a revelation, witnessed something in their psyche that had hitherto remained shrouded' and thus requires analysis so that this new revelation can be 'integrated with existing understanding and feelings. Space has to be made; it has to be fitted in and so everything else has to be re-ordered as a result' (Ellis 2000, 79). Whilst plainly not suggesting that all television viewers have experienced revelations that require the rigours of psychoanalytic therapy, Ellis nevertheless maintains that television:

... finds itself in a similar position. It works over new material for its audiences as a necessary consequence of its position of witness. Television attempts definitions, tries out explanations, creates narratives, talks over, makes intelligible, tries to marginalize, harness speculation, tries to make fit, and, very occasionally, anathemizes.

(Ibid)

We might regard a show like *Gogglebox* as offering an especially acute or 'meta' version of the working through that Ellis describes. Rather than witnessing, contending with, and, in various ways, attempting to make sense of events that occur within the world, *Gogglebox* makes television itself the subject, reviewing the world through revisiting media representation. In the case of the Queen's funeral, the processes of working through that Ellis describes may have already occurred in the original television coverage, whereas *Gogglebox* introduces a further layer of working through by offering an additional set of responses to that coverage (from the groups of families and friends with the show). Writing towards the end of the twentieth century, Ellis is referring mainly to broadcast television and, specifically, news programming, which he regards in the following way: 'The essence of the modern news bulletin lies in speculation about the future just as much as in witness of the common present' (Ibid 75). We might recognise aspects of that description in the original television coverage of the Queen's funeral, which paid meticulous attention to the ceremonial minutiae of the event but also devoted significant time to a consideration of its meaning for the future of the British monarchy and the new King, Charles. In this sense, it can readily be identified as belonging to both the present and future: witnessing and speculating. *Gogglebox*, however, is comfortable in its placement of the funeral ceremony in the past, allowing us to revisit its coverage and the responses of the onscreen families and friends at the time. As a consequence, the immediacy of Ellis' model of working through is diminished to a degree in this alternative process of reflective revisiting. The nature of the working through is also modified somewhat as, tonally, it incorporates humorous responses to events that may have been deemed inappropriate at the time of the original television coverage (and, indeed, there was little humour or irreverence to be found in most of that programming) but finds space to emerge appropriately after even a short passage of time. (And here we can also factor in the distinctions that exist between what might be regarded as the 'official' coverage of the event and a show like *Gogglebox*, which does not possess the same establishment credentials. As a consequence, viewer demographics and audience expectations are likely to deviate.)

The example of the Queen's funeral can be regarded as somewhat extraordinary and atypical for a discussion of *Gogglebox*. Although the show does look back on coverage of news and current affairs on television, the passing of a monarch self-evidently represents a far more significant and potentially disruptive occurrence, so more closely resembling the profile of the kind of 'revelation' in psychoanalytic theory that Ellis' model of working through derives from. Because events of that scale and nature are relatively rare, *Gogglebox* is more likely to concern itself with the more 'ordinary' composition of television programming, and thus reflect upon genres like drama, comedy, lifestyle, sport, films shown on TV, and so on. This is perhaps a more characteristic portrait of the show's interests, as television revisiting television through audience response and, while it may be regarded as less impactful or even trivial, nevertheless represents a re-versioning of Ellis' 'working through' concept. That working through might therefore be seen to function at a lower level or at a stage removed, compared with the news programming Ellis is interested in primarily, and is always framed within the past tense, as content that has already occurred and a viewing experience that is being repeated for entertainment (hence recurring phrases like 'this week, we watched ...' in the voiceover). And, so, the show employs a structure of repeat as the catalyst for a type of working through, as the responses of the family and friendship groups offer a reading of televisual events, reflecting upon them, making sense of them, and evaluating them. It might be said that, in doing so, *Gogglebox* offers an idealised or even nostalgic version of television viewing, in which unified households watch the same shows together and, moving broader still, a nation shares in the same experiences (as represented by the regionally and socially diverse groups in the show). Such discussions have potential merit, and elsewhere it may be useful to consider whether more recent, fragmented viewing practices (such as individuals watching alone and 'self-scheduling') necessarily lead to the abandonment of older, more unified habits (such as domestic groups watching shows together at scheduled times). Nevertheless, *Gogglebox* seems dedicated to a form of collective working through: going over past experiences through group interactions, and finding sense and meaning through talk. Whilst this process marks a deviation from the present and future tense associations that Ellis identifies in his discussion of working through on television, *Gogglebox* does respond to the contemporary television-viewing environment in other ways. Although it is always looking back, the past is also almost always retrievable as long as the shows being discussed remain available digitally through catch-up and streaming services. And so, although arguably a less prominent feature within *Gogglebox*, a reflection upon the past can potentially function to shape future television experiences for some viewers. In this respect, structural repetition can also incorporate forward motion, providing momentum to inform and underpin progress in certain ways.

Notes

1 It is worth mentioning that Silverstone continues this passage with a consideration of 'television as medium,' and 'television as entertainer and informer.' These are important related points that, for reasons of economy and direct pertinence, I have not been able to include here.
2 This story appears in the online incarnation of the *Daily Mail*, *Mail Online* and, consequently, reader comments are posted in response to the themes covered. These comments, according to the site, are un-moderated and so, presumably, are a genuine and unbiased repre-sentation of readers' views. The vast majority are negative about repeats on the BBC, very often relating this to the cost of the com-pulsory license (which every owner of a television in the UK is obliged to pay), so continuing the rhetorical thrust of the original story.
3 Aherne provided the voiceover before her death in 2016. The casting of Cash and Aherne established a clear and self-conscious link with the show they wrote and starred in, *The Royle Family* (BBC, 1998-2012), which will be discussed later in this book, and whose comedic style and format can be regarded as an influence for *Gogglebox*'s focus upon living room inertia, television watching, and the rhythms of humorous everyday speech.

3 Repetition, Television, and Value

If the previous chapter has laid out some of the relationships that can be discovered between repetition and television, drawing in a range of sources that have pursued those connections, we might profitably turn our attention to the matter of considering these associations in detail. One approach to this might involve a reflection upon the potential merits of discussing repetition in relation to television at all and, furthermore, how this may intersect with notions of value that can be attached to the study of this theme and this medium. Whilst not wanting to fall into a somewhat limited commentary upon what could constitute 'good' or 'bad' examples of repetition in television, it is nevertheless useful to think through some of the ways in which we might incorporate critical appreciation into our reflections. This may, in part, represent an effort to avoid any study becoming defined by a passive tone, whereby we simply present an account of something as worthy of attention purely because it exists. Moving on from that basic concern, however, I would also contend that it useful to consider how we can value repetition and television, both in terms of their independence and interrelationship, as a means of providing foundational purpose and direction for the arguments provided.

Evaluating Repetition

There is, of course, no reason why repetition should be regarded as any more valuable a concern than the limitless multitude of alternatives that can be pursued in relation to television. Likewise, no interest that we select will exist in isolation to others and, instead, can form one component within an interconnected and interrelated pattern of associations. Indeed, an alternate study might profitably place a different accent upon some of the suggestions made thus far in this work and, as a consequence, concentrate upon notions of variation in sustained detail, perhaps recognising a close relationship to repetition in doing so (just as this study of repetition has acknowledged a fundamental connection to variation). By placing a weight of emphasis upon any one area of

DOI: 10.4324/9781003265283-4

interest, however, it might be said that we are suggesting implicitly that there are merits in such an approach: that it has value. Any ultimate judgement will be shared between the reader and the writer, of course, and there is naturally an underlying question of whether any sense of worth will find correspondence between the two parties.

However, thinking about value in relation to repetition does raise other questions. We might want to ask, for example, whether one form of repetition can be perceived as more valuable than another, and therefore merits attention to a greater extent. An instinctive response might be that, straightforwardly, this has to be the case; that insisting otherwise might lead to a suggestion of bland uniformity, whereby all forms possess equally matched attributes without variation or texture. And yet, any attempt to distinguish between 'good' or 'bad' repetition, whether in television or any other art form, has the potential to become a complex undertaking. Bruce Kawin touches upon the notion that some kinds of repetition might be better than others as he attempts, concurrently, to introduce a degree of rigour in the types of terminology we employ in relation to the topic. In particular, he sets out a distinction between 'repetitious' and 'repetitive':

> *Repetitious*: when a word, percept or experience is repeated with less impact at each recurrence; repeated to no particular end, out of failure of invention or sloppiness of thought.

> *Repetitive*: when a word, percept or experience is repeated with equal or greater force at each occurrence.

> (Kawin, 4)

These distinctions certainly have the potential to introduce criteria that might lead to value judgements of particular works employing structures of repetition, with those that are regarded as *repetitive* deemed of greater worth than those that are classed as *repetitious*. And, on the surface, these seem like reasonable claims, based on the descriptions that Kawin is offering. If the 'repetitious' is indicative of a 'failure of invention or sloppiness of thought' and to be 'repetitive' leads to 'equal or greater force at each occurrence,' we might reasonably be satisfied that one state is significantly more satisfactory than the other. However, were we to think about the distinctions that Kawin establishes in little more detail, we might conceivably question whether, for example, it is necessarily possible, let alone obvious, to distinguish between the 'repetitious' and the 'repetitive' and whether, in practice, the dividing boundaries between those distinctions are always firmly defined. Television, I would suggest, represents a pertinent case study in this respect (although, in making that claim, I am not recommending it above other media that might prove equally appropriate). Television shows have the capacity to surprise and surpass certain expectations or preconceptions we hold. A structure or format that initially appears unpromising, formulaic, uninventive or even sloppy, can turn out to be insightful, engaging, well-conceived or precise. Possibly the reverse is also true. And, of course, television shows can be experienced differently by different people. We might think back to Helena from *Gogglebox*'s impatient reaction to the Royal piper in the televised coverage, 'It's taking a while, int' it? Really. It's taking a bit of a while, this,' whilst her parents were contrastingly affected by the poignancy of the spectacle as they perceived it. For Helena, the extended scene offering little variation perhaps represented something repetitious yet, for her parents, these qualities contributed to its poetic impact and made it positively repetitive: growing more powerful through its sameness.

In extending his points about the 'repetitious' and the 'repetitive,' Kawin moves to consider some pertinent and, ostensibly, well-chosen examples:

> Successful repetition depends both on the inherent interest of the recurring unit and its context. Thus we come to aesthetics. Some artists are better than others at interesting us in the things they think are worth repeating, or at giving their completed works such life that we will continue to re-experience them with pleasure. I do not enjoy Mozart's French Horn Concertos less at each hearing because I have heard them before; nor do I scold Lear that he has made his point, the last four *nevers* are unnecessary. On the contrary: Lear's cries attain an intensity possible only in unremitting repetition; it is the power of his howl that is under discussion here, and its tendency ... to open on areas of experience generally considered inaccessible to language.
>
> (Ibid, 4–5)

Here, we are returning again to questions of value. Kawin is effectively maintaining that some things are *worth* repeating and that this is certainly the case with regard to the work of a genius like Mozart or Shakespeare, in which Kawin identifies elements (the 'recurring unit' itself and its 'context') that possess 'inherent interest.' I would not wish to contest these points (although, of course, audience responses may diverge on hearing a piece of music many times, just as audiences can exhibit different levels of not only enjoyment but also patience for Lear's repeated lines). However, with television in mind, I am aware that a substantial amount of content that has repetition as a structuring or expressive feature does not enjoy the same artistic status and critical consensus as a Mozart composition or a Shakespeare play. Can repetition be entrusted only to genius artists? That does not seem, to me at least, representative of its manifestations in television (or anywhere else, in fact), which brings us back to the question of the medium's capacity to surprise: of engaging or affecting repetition existing within texts that might, on the surface, appear formulaic or uninspiring. (Perhaps some audiences approach the work of Mozart of Shakespeare with few preconceptions, or even negative expectations, but the cultural status of these figures makes such an occurrence at least less likely.) This brings me to the example of a television show that I'd like to consider in a little more detail: *Great Canal Journeys* (Channel 4, 2014–2021). This show featured the actors and married couple, Timothy West and Prunella Scales until they left in 2020 to be replaced by the actors and friends, Sheila Hancock and Gyles Brandreth.

I would like to focus briefly on a one-off episode of the show, first aired on 20 October 2020, entitled 'The British Isles.' Ostensibly, the episode takes the form of a compilation package of previously-filmed material from earlier series, depicting past boat journeys and assembled around the central narrative theme of West and Scales' final (televised) trip along the Oxford Canal. Even in this sparse description, we can appreciate that a degree of repetition runs through the episode, as its structure is formed through a process of revisiting and remembering. This kind of repackaged content is hardly remarkable for television, occurring frequently in examples of 'lifestyle' TV (Ouellette 2016), a category to which *Great Canal Journeys* might be said to belong, as they periodically and often uncomplicatedly look back across scenes from the past. In this way, 'The British Isles' episode represents nothing extraordinary and, indeed, might be regarded as formulaic in terms of concept, especially as it belongs to a genre of television that is often characteristically untroubling and gentle.

That is certainly the tone of the episode, as it incorporates short vignettes such as visits to a boatyard, a church, Britain's longest canal tunnel, and the highest aqueduct, and finishing with a celebratory family gathering. Again, quite overtly, these experiences represent moments taken from different episodes of the show, constituting something like a 'greatest hits' package in which pace and progression are markedly calm and benign. Indeed, as all of these events have happened already in previous episodes, they are referred to in the past tense and the viewer is untroubled as we're invited to revisit them with West and Scales (with, presumably, anyone who has seen those previous instalments enacting a process of revisitation for themselves). Within the structure of the episode, however, other forms of repetition are evoked and played out. One of these is the recurring convention of West speaking to a member or members of the (off-camera) production team as he steers the vessel. These interludes often concern Scales' medical condition: she has Alzheimer's disease, which has clearly affected their lives together. The experience of boating has remained a pleasure for them as the disease has progressed, continuing their many years of experience together on the canals. Speaking to the camera, West reflects repeatedly on his wife's condition, and these moments are often prompted by shots of Scales herself.

Figure 3.1 Great Canal Journeys.

Figure 3.2 Great Canal Journeys.

Indeed, one earlier example of these monologues in the episode features footage of West speaking about Scales' increasing deafness, intercut with images of Scales repeatedly, sitting silently at the front of the boat. This physical connection is given further thematic resonance as West describes the distance that this illness has created within their relationship:

> It has got worse. A big step back, I think, was when she began to be really quite deaf. It does make conversation very difficult. So, we

don't talk to each other as much as we did, and that's sad and ... and awful really. We've been instantaneously swapping ideas and feelings for a large number of years but ... and now we can't. I do feel quite lonely sometimes, and it's having an effect on my own mind, certainly. I haven't got people to ... to share things with and that means my own brain is slowing up. Which is ... annoying.

As the sequence lengthens in duration, the camera undertakes a passive scrutiny of West's description, as he in turn demonstrates an awareness of his own relationship to the camera, striking a slightly uneasy balance between a direct, honest, and expressive account of their life together, and management of the emotion he is willing or able to display on screen. As a result, his delivery is at times understated, and there are pauses as he considers briefly how best to convey certain aspects of their position whilst remaining articulate and composed. Running underneath this effort, however, is tension as West equally contends with the experienced reality of what he is describing, and how it is impacting upon him even as he relays it in level, measured terms. Consequently, very small details like a genial smile, an intake of breath, a tight closing of eyes, or a glance away from the camera can become underscored with a form of strain, wordlessly conveying the weight that bears down upon them.

The intercutting of this speech with the shots of Scales sitting at the front of the boat provides a visual depiction of the small but significant chasm that is slowly opening between the couple, despite their close companionship and devoted love, as the disease claims the further territory. The placement of each at opposite ends of the boat reinforces this psychological notion in physical terms and, as the editing pattern is constructed to suggest that these shots occupy the same time, the sequence invites an interpretation that this partial separation is happening in that moment: that they are already parted as we encounter them in their respective zones. The sheer physical length of the narrowboat itself is employed creatively in this respect, as the show takes advantage of its natural form to develop a poetic pattern of imagery because any couple sitting at either end of the vessel would necessarily be distanced fairly significantly from each other. (We might equally reflect that the boat's dimensions have been capitalised upon in the interview sections with West, as the tight space at the back necessitates close proximity between camera and subject, resulting in a series of tight shots that help to pick out and emphasise the subtle nuances in his expression and appearance.) The idea of increasing detachment is intensified in other audio-visual contrasts that are established and pursued. West and Scales are filmed facing in opposite directions, for example – him looking slightly to the right of the frame, her looking to the left – presenting a delicate and subdued oppositional relationship whereas the simple placement of them angled in the same direction might otherwise have conveyed aspects of their complicity or unity (which is certainly featured elsewhere in the series). A further contrast is introduced in the distinction between West's coherent vocal description against Scales' stillness and silence, which the show sustains and accentuates through shots of her that are held and lingered upon in the edit. One result of this, we might say, is a portrait of two forms of personal dignity bearing up in the face of difficulty: West handling the strain as he attempts a lucid and controlled account of it to the camera; Scales maintaining a quiet and restful poise as they journey along.

These kinds of depictions within the show also place a new kind of strain upon the idea of repetition and the way that it is being represented within the aesthetic and narrative composition. As well as the easy, comforting return to past journeys (both from this series and beyond), we are gradually imbued with an increasing awareness of the vital importance that repetition is now taking on in the lives of West and Scales. As they repeat the routes and routines of past journeys, they contend with and, to some degree, provide a small defence against the realisation that these habits are being lost to them and, ultimately, will no longer remain. The show does not build this into a melodramatic point and, indeed, neither of the couple reflects upon the idea in anything approaching that tone. Instead, apparently passive moments like repeated sequences in which we watch Scales opening lock gates or West steering the boat begin to take on resonance and meaning *through* their repetition, and through their context within the lives of this couple: the life they have had together and the life they have now. The physical repetition of leisurely tasks is bound together with their emotional perspective, and so aesthetic elements that might otherwise possess simple or straightforward traits are given new potency.

Figure 3.3 Great Canal Journeys.

Figure 3.4 Great Canal Journeys.

If the episode contains certain unanticipated revelations, they are embedded within and emerge through an overarching structure of repetition that otherwise conforms uncomplicatedly (and, in some respects, unchallengingly) within the generic boundaries of a lifestyle show offering a recapitulation of previous episodes. Certainly, the disclosure of Scales' Alzheimer's (which hadn't been revealed until filming for *Great Canal Journeys* began) would provide a more intense and poignant focus for the series, but it is notable that the show does not necessarily seek to heighten or exploit the drama that this condition might potentially generate. Indeed, the treatment of Scales' condition, and West's responses to it, are characterised by a subtle and subdued tone, deriving from a desire shared between the couple (we might surmise) to contend with the realities of their situation through measured, practical, and composed responses. As a consequence, the languid rhythms of the show are not disrupted or broken to accommodate a more obviously dramatic element. Instead, Scales and West's reflections take their place within a cyclical pattern of repetition, forming points of unity with the show's overarching and light-handed dedication to retracing and remembering past journeys, within the common generic borders of a 'recap' episode.

It seems unlikely that any emotional weight this episode possesses would be immediately apparent from a broader look at the description of *Great Canal Journeys* within a television schedule or through an online portal. Indeed, the Channel 4 streaming platform provides the following brief summary of this episode: 'Tim and Pru return to the Oxford Canal for a voyage through the beautiful Cherwell Valley, as they recall their favourite waterway trips around the British Isles.' We might reflect that this outline is entirely accurate in terms of the episode's main narrative concerns and that it encapsulates perfectly well the way in which repetition features straightforwardly as a central focal point within its structure ('they recall their favourite waterway trips …'). Equally, however, we might suggest that the words possess a somewhat uninspiring quality, hinting at a formulaic episode design that might be picked up by any amount of series within this genre of programming, especially as they reach the end of a series run. Recalling Kawin's earlier classifications, it might indicate something that is distinctly 'repetitious,' whose impact has already been realised adequately in previous episodes, and whose only attraction would be a rather unimaginative, albeit entertaining, revisiting of the past. Yet, it is precisely this revisiting, and the extent to which that previous footage is arranged and re-presented, that lends new focus and clarity to the lives of Scales and West as they engage with (and re-engage within) the cycles of repetition that the show has constructed. If we return briefly to Kawin's distinctions, then, the 'repetitious' evolves and reveals itself to 'repetitive' after all: occurring again but with greater force. It is only through closer consideration of the television text (as opposed to the broader appraisals of 'television as medium' in the accounts offered by Silverstone, Ellis, Kompare, and Williams, for example) that these kinds of qualities can perhaps be appreciated properly. Furthermore, we can only discover them through a more precise appreciation of the ways in which they are represented in a show's aesthetic composition and, as the example of *Great Canal Journeys* might begin to suggest, by scrutinising aspects of style in relative detail.

Evaluating Television

Recommending the detailed consideration of style within television shows is not without controversy in academic debate, however. It is therefore worth reflecting upon the motivations behind such an approach, what benefits it can offer, and what contentions might be formulated in response to it. One starting point can be found in the work of Jason Jacobs, a key figure in the drive toward the closer scrutiny of television and the more precise consideration of style in relation to achievement. He sets out this position effectively in a seminal 2001 article, 'Issues of judgement and value in television studies':

> We need to recognise that our criteria for judgement are in part derived by defining the nature of our involvement with specific texts. As with the analysis of all art, understanding that involvement requires above all concentrated study: minimally, the close observation of texts in order to support the claims and judgements we may wish to make about them.

> (Jacobs 2001, 430–431)[1]

Elsewhere in his article, Jacobs mentions the tendency to neglect the 'close observation' of television texts derived in part from a conceptualisation of television 'even in its nominally artistic forms, as a relay of something else: sociocultural discourses, patterns of taste, ideology and noxious forms of representation. Much of television studies continue to consider television in this manner, as a relay for something else: like a language' (Jacobs 2001, 429). This description of the 2001 landscape is vital, encapsulating an inherent focus away from the television text's composition in favour of attending to the messages that pass through it, as though it were simply – or at least, primarily – a conduit for meaning. That kind of perception may form barriers against, or at least provide limited capacity for, the formulation of 'claims and judgements' that Jacobs mentions, and so we can see a joining together of a close analysis methodology and critical evaluation that, according to his account, was not readily accommodated in previous practices.

Jacobs' observation that television had been widely regarded as 'like a language' in television studies may refer to the significant influence of semiotics within the discipline,[2] which in turn bears a relationship to the dominance of cultural studies. It is something of a passing remark in the article: intended, surely, to briefly describe a path taken before offering an alternative route. Nevertheless, combined with a further comment regarding canons in Television Studies that appeared in Jacobs' article 'Television Aesthetics: An Infantile Disorder,' a dividing line begins to emerge a little more firmly. In response to Glenn Creeber's concerns that his edited collection *Fifty Key Television Programmes* (Creeber 2004) could risk becoming an exercise in canon-building, Jacobs writes that:

'In the air, I suspect, is the ghost of Pierre Bourdieu and his *Distinction* (1979) (perhaps somewhat reductively), where canons enact a 'symbolic violence' on those with attenuated cultural capital, who then have to accept the self-evident truth of the established hierarchies of taste. My issue with this is as follows: nobody has to pay any attention to canons. They are not [...] natural laws; neither are they legislated for in parliament or a court of law. They are always up for debate – indeed, it is difficult to think of proposing a canon without hundreds of cultural studies scholars jumping on it.'

(Jacobs 2006, 27)

Again, the comment on cultural studies is articulated somewhat briefly but perhaps this brevity intensified a sense of its dismissiveness, which in turn attracted a robust response from self-described 'scholar partly trained in cultural studies,' Matt Hills. He asserts that:

> Jacobs' irritation with 'cultural studies scholars' is palpable [...] And
> his reference to the ghost of Bourdieu seems to impute a phantasmic
> quality or spectral presence/absence to such arguments, coding
> Bourdieuians (and cultural studies scholars) as lacking in good sense
> and as somehow being detached from what is then presented as
> material reality: canons can just be ignored.
>
> (Hills 2011, 110)

Hills does not think that canons can be ignored. Indeed, for him, to
adopt 'a position which disconnects canonicity from all relations of
power seems [...] to be elitist in highly traditional aesthetic terms'
(Ibid, 111). It is worth attending to the anxiety, voiced by Hills, that
offering critical judgements on television might lead to the construction of canons, which are inherently 'elitist in highly traditional aesthetic terms' and therefore implicitly related to older, allegedly non-
progressive practices. It is perhaps notable that, elsewhere, Hills
should tie his notion of 'Traditional aesthetics' back to F.R. Leavis,
and by implication position Jacobs' regard for canons as part of that
critical legacy (Ibid, 110). Hills' linking together of 'Traditional aesthetics' with Leavis and elitism occurs in service to a wider purpose, it
would appear, of defining Jacobs' position on canons as 'harking back'
to pre-Structuralism, rooted in unfashionable or undesirable traits
(moralism or elitism, for example).[3]

Connecting these debates together, we might perceive a relationship
forming between the close appreciation of television style, the
advancement of value judgments, and a contested disquiet regarding
canonisation. Hills, in fact, is generally approving of Jacobs' analytical
approach, especially its focus on textual 'fragments' and, as he perceives
it, a potential relationship to the close readings undertaken within fan
cultures (Ibid, 108–109). Indeed, Hills uses this prospect to propose an
emphasis upon 'popular aesthetics' that would involve 'investigating
how aesthetic judgements are made by all sorts of non-academic audiences' (Ibid, 113).[4]

However, in a later revival of the debate, Helen Piper implicitly rejects
both Jacobs' and Hills' positions, suggesting that: 'any judgement (by
whomsoever it is made) will lack ethical authority unless underpinned by
consensual ideals' (Piper 2016, 167). One interpretation of this statement
would be that no group is entitled to speak unconditionally about
'artistic achievement' in the absence of a consensus on what constitutes
an understanding of 'art' in relation to television (Ibid, 167–168). This,
potentially, is a valuable assertion, and it is certainly true that there can
be slippage in the way that terms such as 'art,' 'aesthetics' and 'style' are
sometimes used in television studies. I think we would struggle to dis-
agree with the suggestion that examining those terms more closely, or

even tightening their usage, might benefit critical understanding.[5] (The desire for consensus may prove difficult to satisfy, though, and such an effort might open up equally fruitful debates about the apparently unending disparities over what constitutes 'art.')

Piper focuses specifically upon style when she draws together a rejection of value judgements in academia, a perceived privileging of American serial television in academic debate, and her case for a more sustained consideration of the local and national (or 'home') in accounts of television:

> It may be objected that I am conflating popularity with value, but it seems legitimate to question how it is that an American TV series such as *Mad Men* (the seventh and most recent series of which garnered a mere 0.2% audience share in the UK, a 'meagre' 28,500 viewers [footnote omitted]) can justify quite so much establishment interest from British academic critics, whilst the 'greatest drama hits' of Britain's most watched channels gather domestic audiences that are immense by comparison but attract virtually none [footnote omitted]. None of these ignored programmes strike me as unworthy of aesthetic interest, but their aesthetic accomplishments do not necessarily survive extrapolation from the context of viewing. They are, to put it simply, as much about 'home' as they are about style.
>
> (Ibid, 181–182)

Here, Piper usefully and legitimately questions why a type (and, indeed, nationality) of television should receive critical devotion within academic debate. One ambition for scholarly inquiry, we might presume, is that it could strive to encompass a wide range of programming and, in doing so, maintain an awareness and appreciation of the useful distinctions that exist between shows of varying types, developing an understanding of their particularity in the process. Christine Geraghty, in a key essay exploring questions of aesthetics in relation to television drama, attends to these kinds of points directly:

> I would like to think *more broadly* about aesthetics, in particular making connections between film and television rather than defining them against each other, and also to think *more narrowly* about the object we are trying to analyse, to think about television drama without trying to fit quiz shows and sport, for example, into a single account [italics in original].
>
> (Geraghty 2003, 29)

I would suggest that a profitable relationship can be established between Piper's entreaty for more attention to be paid to 'ignored programmes' and Geraghty's suggestion that we approach different types of pro-gramming with an understanding of their inherent differences, so avoiding a tendency to speak in broad terms about 'television' as though all of its content were uniform (a point that Geraghty attends to else-where in her argument). There is indeed no reason why a type of show, or shows from different national contexts, should not be a focus for critical interest but, in acknowledging the disparities between these shows, we may need to adjust the ways in which we approach and evaluate them.

However, Piper's following assertion that '"the greatest drama hits" of Britain's most watched channels' are 'to put it simply, as much about "home" as they are about style' is equally worth considering. Specifically, we might pursue the question of how a television show can be 'about' style a little more closely. 'Home' can certainly be a potent thematic interest, expressed variously by shows in different ways, but style cannot be applied selectively in the same manner. Style is innate to all shows, of whatever type. As a consequence, placing 'home' alongside 'style' could never create a like-for-like comparison, meaning that the terms would not exist on an equal footing in critical debate, or be interchangeable as equivalents. It is quite possible, of course, to move the weight of emphasis away from a consideration of style when discussing television, and this path has cer-tainly been pursued in television studies scholarship. However, this does present certain issues when it comes to describing elements within a show itself, even minimally, because such an endeavour will always involve an engagement, however nominal, with style: the way that the work has conveyed its themes through compositional choice.

This problem is illustrated in Piper's article when she needs to describe a sequence from the British television drama *Happy Valley* (BBC 2014-) to draw out points regarding the representation of 'local and national anxieties' in that show (Piper, 178). Piper acknowledges that the example is 'nominal' and 'too brief' (Ibid), and it is certainly the case that the sequence is given sparse consideration, but it does still include mention of shot types, framing, and editing. The issue, however, is whether this minimal account adequately supports Piper's contentions that the sequence is an 'affective representation of [central character, Catherine's] working through of the trauma,' that it offers 'a chance to share a rare gulp of fresh air and a glimpse of the horizon' or that 'the alignment with Catherine's insider view of the town offers a native rather than a tourist view of a very British *and* specifically Yorkshire landscape [italics in original]' (Ibid). Such claims rest upon the ways in which the scene has been constructed and conveyed – its style – which create qualities like affect or alignment within the drama. In the absence of precise and detailed engagement with stylistic choices, there is a risk that we might simply be asked to take Piper's word for it.

We are moving to the relatively straightforward point, then, that television shows of all varieties will always be 'about' style at an intrinsic level because it is impossible to extricate audio-visual design from thematic content. It is the case, however, that style would never be a uniform quality across all shows, meaning that standardised criteria for evaluating style would always be difficult to arrive at, if not impossible. Whether we choose to engage with style or not is a question of critical discrimination, but turning away from style would always be an act of conscious omission. Style cannot disappear from television, any more than content can.

These issues become pertinent within a study of repetition and television, and to the progression of this book. The following chapters suggest repetition to be central in the expression of key themes but, at the same time, the discussion is necessarily concerned with how forms of repetition and other related thematic concerns are conveyed through stylistic choices: what we see and hear. For the reasons outlined above, I would suggest this to be a practical basis for discussing television texts in detail. It is also the case that, as the three following chapters attend to just six television shows, a process of selection has clearly taken place. Of course, the incorporation and evocation of repetition within these shows has been a major guiding factor in their inclusion, but these examples have also been chosen because, to my mind, they develop relationships with forms of repetition that are meaningful and significant. As a result, I am proposing that these shows are valuable, that they represent achievement and merit close attention. Implicitly, then, I am affording them an elevated status: in the unlikely event that a canon of shows featuring repetition were to be attempted, it is possible that I would place this group near the top. However, I share Jacobs's ambivalence towards canons, and I would endorse a wider application of Andrew Klevan's recommendation regarding aesthetic criticism, that it 'should be respectful towards canons, but also productively antagonistic' (Klevan 2018, 96).

The selection is also fairly narrow in terms of type: comedies and dramas. I am conscious that these genres have attracted perhaps the most critical attention in academic writing about television, possibly at the expense of others. I am equally aware that varieties of television outside of comedy and drama – sports, quiz, news, reality, soap opera, and food, for example – often contain strong elements of repetition (and, indeed, my discussion of shows like *Gogglebox* and *Great Canal Journeys* has already made a connection with other genres). I am not suggesting that these other kinds of shows do not represent achievement, or that they are not valuable but, instead, that the shows I have selected for extended consideration demonstrate depth and richness in their engagement with repetition; this is part of their achievement. At

the same time, the range of shows discussed is limited to British pro-
ductions or co-productions from the last five decades. Television did
not begin in the 1980s and, if there is a perceived neglect of earlier
periods in scholarly work, this book perhaps risks contributing to it. I
would simply add that I can see no reason why any future studies of
repetition could not work within different parameters, and I would
welcome that development. Similarly, I am not seeking to endorse
shows produced by a particular nation and I can say with confidence
that my selection of case studies is not influenced by any sense of their
'Britishness.' Whilst there are nods to a specific national context in
each of the shows (from 1990s television culture in *The Royle Family* to
the National Health Service in *This is Going to Hurt*, for example), I
am interested in their handling of the more universal theme of repetition: how it is incorporated within narratives, how it relates to other
underlying concerns, and how it is expressed stylistically. That would
be the case wherever the shows were set and produced and, if there is
something particular about repetition in British television, the notion
is not explored in my account.

Notes

1 Jacobs' article is wide-ranging and, consequently, has been influential
  in several areas of television studies. However, its explicit and detailed
  engagement with, indeed, issues of judgement and value makes it a
  crucial influence (arguably, *the* crucial influence) within the move towards television aesthetics that occurred from the turn of the century
  onwards.
2 John Fiske and John Hartley's influential 1978 book, *Reading
  Television*, provide a crystallisation of this trend when reflecting on
  some limitations of objective, quantitative content analysis (which has
  equally endured within television studies): 'content analysis does not
  help us to respond to the individual programme, nor, more importantly, the viewing session; it does not help us with matters of interpretation nor with how we respond to the complex significance and
  subtleties of the television text. That sort of reading of television
  requires that we move beyond the strictly objective and quantitative
  methods of content analysis and into the newer and less well explored
  discipline of semiotics.' (Fiske and Hartley, 2004 (1978]: 21).
3 As it turns out, Jacobs is more than comfortable with his definition as
  'a pre-structuralist Arnoldian of some sort' and, presumably, similarly
  unconcerned with connections to Leavis as he suggests: 'if you really
  want to peg my approach it would be a species of practical criticism,
  with close reading as its method.' (Jacobs, 2014).
4 Without wishing to diminish that ambition in the absence of a thor-
  ough engagement with its merits, it is nevertheless prudent to note that
  fan cultures are a major focus of Hills' academic work and, indeed, he

ends his article with a final sentence directing readers to a book of his own that deals with 'production/fan/academic discourses' in *Doctor Who* (Hills: 116).

5 On this theme, Sarah Cardwell provides a rigorous exploration of the aesthetics-led approach in television studies within her chapter 'Television aesthetics: Stylistic analysis and beyond,' which incorporates a consideration of how broadly the term 'aesthetics' can be applied within the discipline and recommends opportunities for greater distinction and definition (Cardwell, 2013: 23-44).

4 Repetition and Relationships

We can think about television content in terms of the relationships that are established and explored. Such considerations might incorporate the relationships that are constructed between the arrangement of aesthetic elements within a show, such as lighting, set, camera position and movement, performance, props, and so on. We might then extend this to reflect upon the ways in which relationships between people are illustrated and investigated within that composition. Almost all television shows, we might reasonably conclude, are about human relationships – the often-intricate interactions that take place within groups and between individuals – and consequently, the way in which people are presented to us within an arrangement of aesthetic features becomes a significant and influencing concern. An understanding of the relationships between people on screen is affected crucially by their relationship to that aesthetic presentation. If we pursue that kind of awareness, we can attend equally to the relationship that we, as viewers, are forming with the television show, precisely as a consequence of those relationships presented to us onscreen. And, so, we might perceive relationships functioning on three interrelated levels: the relationships between people in a show, which are framed within the relationships between aesthetic elements, which impacts ultimately upon the relationships we develop with that show.

Acknowledging the centrality of relationships within television is useful, I would suggest when we are attending to the expressive handling and creative employment of repetition as a thematic interest within shows. We can ask, for example, how repetition becomes embedded within the network of relationships that television shows establish and, furthermore, how it is afforded meaning and significance within such configurations. To this end, we might develop a focus on the ways in which repetition interacts with the kinds of relationships described briefly, to the extent that it might become a structuring feature. In this chapter, I want to centre these kinds of concerns around two examples: *The Royle Family* (BBC 1998–2012) and *The Trip* (BBC 2010–2014; Sky 2017–2020).

DOI: 10.4324/9781003265283-5

Although these shows may have certain features in common, they nevertheless provide distinct and idiosyncratic illustrations of the interests I have begun to lay out. Thus, while interesting resonances may occur between them, selecting them for extended attention should not suggest an attempt to establish a standard or uniform way in which repetition and relationships manifest within television in any general sense.

The Royle Family

Aspects of repetition are entrenched within the spatial arrangement and dynamic of *The Royle Family* from the outset. This can be attributed, in part, to particular creative decisions that were taken regarding the setting and location, which provided a contrast to certain orthodox approaches within situation comedy at the time. As Amy Holdsworth notes:

> The critically acclaimed and much-loved series broke the conventions of British situation comedy in the late 1990s. Set in a Manchester living room, the mundane reality of this ordinary working-class family was captured by the observational style of the comedy. The action rarely left the space of the living room, though it occasionally ventured to the kitchen, and at the heart of the family was the television.
>
> (Holdsworth 2011, 17)[1]

As episodes of the show progress, this sparse assortment of dramatic spaces creates an underlying pattern of repetitions, literally confining where interactions can take place but also creating locations for familial and familiar congregation. It is appropriate that Holdsworth should conclude her description with the observation that the television is at the 'heart' of the family because, indeed, an abundance of scenes take place with the Royles congregated around the set in their living room, and this is the most repeated composition within the show. Indeed, Holdsworth's account of the show incorporates its title sequence, which depicts the family gathered in front of their television: 'Whilst some things change, some things stay the same, and each time we still return to the preserved portrait of the family in the title sequence' (Ibid, 19), indicating a form of perpetuating recurrence within elements of its overall framing structure.

The limited range of dramatic locales within *The Royle Family* impacts, understandably, upon the scale and range of events that take place within the show, effectively narrowing them but, in turn, giving the show a particular intensity. James Zborowski has pointed out that the show 'does not only capture, or represent, the everyday, but becomes a programme *about* how the everyday is *structured*, a reflexive feat it achieves in part by being about the everyday activity that viewers must participate in if they are to be a viewer' (Zborowski 2013, 128). The show is alert to the notion that recurrence becomes a key facet within this structuring and, indeed, in the episode, we are going to be considering in a little more detail (the third episode of series two), father Jim Royle (Ricky Tomlinson) makes a gentle sarcastic reference to this when his daughter, Denise (Caroline Aherne) and partner Dave (Craig Cash) arrive at the house: 'Bloody hell, that's the last thing we want: Torville and Dean back again, eh? Sit down kids. I haven't seen you two since, erm … When was the last time I saw you two?... Must have been, er, last night wasn't it? Bloody hell!' Even though *The Royle Family*'s dramatic patterning is hardly committed to climactic events, these lines nevertheless have a particularly transitional quality, marking the entrance of two characters and reinforcing Jim's frequent mode of interaction with family members. Yet, equally, his words illustrate not only the show's dedication to instances of repeating action but also the extent to which it is especially confident and comfortable with this as an underlying, even defining quality. To extend Zborowski's observations regarding reflexivity, the show declares in understated tones that the shape of these characters' everyday lives incorporates repetition strongly, to the extent that they can reference this self-consciously (through Jim), and furthermore that our investment as viewers will involve engaging with that element: that, to use Zborowski's terminology, this is an aspect of the everyday that we 'must participate in.'

Indeed, a yet more casual and jokey reference to the show's repetitions exists just before Dave and Denise arrive. Jim and wife Barbara (Sue Johnston) have been watching an episode of *Changing Rooms* (BBC 1996–2004) on television, much to Jim's vocalised displeasure, which is hosted by a presenter called Carole Smilie. With Barbara dispatched to greet their guests (because another aspect of the show's repetitions involves Jim's consistent lack of physical activity in contrast to Barbara's kinetic bursts) Jim reflects in a quiet undertone to himself: 'Smilie, my arse.' Jim frequently uses this turn of phrase within the show, applying 'my arse' as an almost automatic reflex to the end of many different statements and sentences. To this extent, it might well be regarded as a catchphrase, conventional within many comedy formats, and that is probably how it is generally and uncomplicatedly perceived. Yet, as we can see with Jim's utterance in this instance, it often occurs more as incidental punctuation or fleeting reflection rather than being worked into the delivery of a comedically-impactful moment. Even when heard by other characters, it has the potential to be remarked upon or not, and as a consequence simply becomes part of the fabric of repetitions that the show creates, and which become integrated into character attitudes and behaviours. It is not difficult, therefore, to understand the recurring 'my arse' line as an instance of *The Royle Family* referencing its own dramatic structures and, specifically, its repetitions.

Denise and Dave make their way into the room and sit down on the sofa alongside Barbara, with Jim positioned in his own chair to the right of the frame. Here, we can appreciate an aspect of visual repetition within the show being evoked, complementing those vocal references that have been made up to this point. The arrangement of characters within this space is consistent across episodes and even the ordering of Dave, Denise, and Barbara on the sofa (seated left to right in that order) remains unchanged, with additional characters such as Nana (Liz Smith) integrated simply into that formation when they feature. The actors within the scene demonstrate an awareness of and respond physically to this repeated formation as Cash, Aherne and Johnston each assume a posture that remains enduringly constant.[2] They allow their bodies to sink into the soft L-shape of the furniture, angling their frames into semi-reclining positions, and letting their heads prop comfortably against the upright cushions behind them. Filmed in *The Royle Family*'s single-camera setup, this composition is returned to again and again from slightly varying aspects and distances as episodes progress, which not only serves to reinforce its inherent settled, and unchanging uniformity but also results in its ultimately becoming a repeated visual motif within the frame and across the show's accumulated hours. Although Jim is ostensibly separated from this arrangement, positioned in his own chair away from the group of three, his own physical posture complements and mirrors that of his family members, as he too sits low in the furniture with his head propped up slightly. In this episode, a recurring shot incorporates Jim as a visual element alongside the family group within the frame, creating a pattern of resemblances between the complementary shapes of his, Dave, Denise, and Barbara's bodies.

Figure 4.1 The Royle Family.

In this way, he is made part of the same group despite instances in which his words and actions are intended to make him distinct from them, particularly those moments in which he positions himself as an antagonistic presence in conversation through the interjection of sarcastic or even insulting comments.

The shared seated postures of the family group can be regarded as an especially understated quality within scenes from *The Royle Family*, occurring as an almost unconscious instinct for each of the characters and inherently possessing a non-declaratory quality as each essentially settle back into their relaxed poses. We could, therefore, easily miss the complicity that is established within the group. Similarly, this lack of pronouncement might cause us to overlook the fact that they are mirroring each other's postures, that a particular pose is being repeated back and forth between them. This is important, however, as a means of appreciating the way in which repetition is being incorporated visually into a composition of sympathetic alignment among the characters. It becomes a foundational shaping structure for interactions between them so that if Barbara sits forward to light a cigarette, accentuate a point or admire the hem of Denise's trousers, she can return effortlessly to the settled configuration. The arrangement of characters along the sofa, extending to Jim, emphasises the repetition inherent in this composition and, indeed, when the Royle's son Anthony (Ralf Little) enters the scene and sits in the chair to the left of the main sofa, he continues the line of repeated association in the other direction (and forms a relationship with Jim's position on the other side, which will be discussed later).

These aspects of visual composition contribute strongly to the tone and mood of scenes and, indeed, frame the nature of the relationships that exist between these characters. We are presented with a portrait of mutual comfort and ease, assured of the fact it is important for these characters to experience such sensations with each other, and to share them (albeit unconsciously) through traits such as reciprocated posture. These qualities become a foundation for any potential deviations or even tensions that may occur within the group, as the anchoring physical composition can always be (and always is) returned to. In this episode, the emphasis on comfort leads to an instance of repetitive behaviour that is, significantly, distributed among the group. They have been discussing Anthony's new girlfriend, Emma (Sheridan Smith), and, with Barbara having mentioned unrelatedly that she resembles a Spice Girl and has her nose pierced, Jim rounds off the discussion with a characteristically derogatory put-down, labelling Emma 'Piggy Spice' (a reference to the 1990s female pop group, The Spice Girls). The family chuckles mildly at this and there follows a silence between them as their collective gaze rests once again up the television set (a view replicated for us as the camera is positioned in a half-reverse shot between the sofa and Jim's chair, and directed towards the TV screen). The only sound is a contented inward sigh from Barbara, until we move to a two-shot of Dave and Denise as Denise says: 'Dave, why don't you take your coat off?' He replies 'I'm alright' but, instead of this constituting a concluding response to the exchange, there follows a somewhat extended discussion of the matter, with other family members contributing as it persists:

Denise: You may as well take it off, Dave.
Dave: It's alright. I'm OK.
           (Pause)
Denise: Why don't you just take it off?
Dave: I'm fine with it on.
Barbara: Take your jacket off, Dave.
Dave: I'm OK Barbara.
Barbara: You won't feel the benefit, you know, when you go out.
Dave: Doesn't matter.
Denise: Why don't you just take it off?
Jim: Take your bloody jacket off will you, Dave!
           (Dave leans forward and removes his jacket.)
Dave: Bloody hell.
Jim: 'Bloody hell's right.
           (Having removed his jacket, Dave reclines back into the sofa.)
Dave: I was alright there with that on.
Barbara: That's better.
Denise: See?
           (Dave sighs and shakes his head gently.)

The replicating circularity of this exchange is clearly integral to its humorous effect: the elevating of a distinctly trivial and mundane subject to the extent that it receives an incongruous intensity and depth of focus through constant re-articulation. It is little wonder that Dave is left mildly exasperated when the conclusion finally arrives. *The Royle Family* is adept at finding humour in the uneventful details of everyday life, with moments such as this emerging from an otherwise inconsequential comment or observation. The motivation for Denise, Barbara, and finally Jim repeating the same request is not necessarily fixed around a single purpose: Denise may be bothered by the visual detail of Dave still wearing a coat indoors, Barbara may be drawing upon conventional wisdom that wearing a coat indoors means an individual 'won't feel the benefit' when they go out later, and Jim may simply seek a resolution to an irritating conversation and uses repetition as a means of achieving that. However, combining their repeated entreaties, we can observe a shared emphasis upon the idea of comfort and conformity: that Dave would at some stage be more contented if he were to remove the garment now and, equally, that his appearance would consequently align yet more thoroughly with the other members of the household (none of whom are wearing coats). In this respect, we can perhaps recognise an effort towards achieving, to an even greater degree, the kind of physical affinity that exists already between the group in their shared physical postures. It would seem entirely appropriate, therefore, that this endeavour should in turn involve them falling into a vocal replication of each other's words, revolving around the same spoken theme just as their bodily poses are mirrored and repeated between them. And, indeed, as Dave returns to his semi-reclined seating position on the sofa once his coat has been removed, he uncomplicatedly re-joins the line of resemblance that the show has established between its characters.

There is a brief flurry of activity when the group register that Anthony is being dropped off by his girlfriend, Emma, with Dave and Denise moving across the room to crouch at the front window, viewing the scene of the couple's parting (and narrating the events to Barbara and Jim, who have not moved). This relative peak in excitement eventually dissipates, however, and, having entered the living room, Anthony is despatched to the kitchen to make cups of tea for everyone. This represents a comedic recurrence within the show, as though no one else is capable or inclined to make the tea, and it is worth reflecting that even this small detail represents a further instance of repetition being entrenched within the rhythms and structures of this household, as Anthony is consequently called upon to perform the duty routinely (to the extent that, of course, it becomes a running joke). To accompany the tea, he brings out a biscuit barrel and each family member selects their particular choice. As he unwraps his 'Club' biscuit, Dave spontaneously breaks into song, with a rendition of the theme tune from the television advertisement for the snack, which was culturally familiar at the time of the episode's broadcast. This prompts Jim to respond by singing the theme for the 'Penguin' advertisement, matching the chocolate biscuit he has selected and, finally, Barbara performs the song from the advertisement for 'Flake' chocolate bars, even though she too is holding up a 'Club' biscuit like Dave's. The direction of the singing, therefore, travels in a circular motion, starting with Dave before transferring to Jim and then returning back to Barbara. We might note, again, an activity being repeated within and between the group and that the subject of this process is, in itself, a repetition of song lyrics that are already widely known and understood, hence their immediate recognition within the scene. It would be tempting, perhaps, to read the moment as simply another illustration within *The Royle Family* of mundanity being displayed and explored, possibly for subtle comedic effect. Yet, the family members' act of repeating promotional songs back to each other also seems to work as a means of embellishing and extending another instance of shared complicity, providing further points of aligned experience and understanding within their communal consumption of the chocolate biscuits. Again, it is perhaps striking that the show seeks almost incessantly to work in layers of repetition in its depiction of these characters, using these as a catalyst to underscore the defining relationships that exist between them.

The references to these television adverts prompt a further association for Jim and he sings a much older theme from the television advertisement for the 'Nimble' bread loaf brand (which Dave correctly identifies when Jim playfully tests him). From here, there follows a passage of visual representation that is, on the one hand, somewhat asserted in terms of the framing choices that have been selected and, on the other, undramatic in terms of the subject depicted. The camera begins in close-up on Jim's face as he munches on his chocolate biscuit and says 'correct, young man' in response to Dave's successful identification of the 'Nimble' advert. From here, we pan left and tilt down to Jim's right hand, holding his biscuit in its wrapper, and this motion continues as we continue to travel left and arrive at Barbara on the sofa. The camera settles for a moment as she unwraps her biscuit and eats it by letting it pass between her lips, the chocolate coating melting in her mouth. As she performs this action, she closes her eyes in a display of pleasure and, when she opens them again, she has tilted her head towards Denise, seated next to her. Barbara emits a low sigh of satisfaction, and the camera follows the direction of her eyeline, panning across left to Denise as she looks back at her mother and makes the same, deep sighing noise.

Figure 4.2 The Royle Family.

The two acknowledge each other's contentment through this exchange of replicated looks and sounds, and there is even a moment in which they vocalise their pleasure in unison. Once again, the camera is still for a moment as it rests upon Denise's face, and she turns her head away from Barbara to watch the television whilst eating her own biscuit. But then the panning left continues as she turns to look at Dave, seated on her right, lifts her chocolate bar towards him, and he looks back at her. Dave emits his own slightly more abrupt and heavier sigh of gratification, as though he had been aware of the exchange between Denise and Barbara, understood its conventions, and now adds in his own contribution (replete with a little nod of the head to demonstrate his agreement with their shared sentiments). The camera continues its journey of panning left in close-up, moving on from Dave to Anthony as he voraciously finishes his own biscuit, ramming a large section of it into his mouth and screwing the wrapper up in his hand as he watches the television and balances his mug of tea on his chest. We stay with Anthony as he munches enthusiastically, sniffing occasionally, until Jim interjects with his thoughts on the best advert of all time, and we cut to a wider shot of the family group, with only the son omitted from the frame.

This cut to the wider shot effectively demarcates the previous configuration of panning close-ups as a sequence, distinguished by its own aesthetic characteristics and, in fact, set apart from the general filming style of this episode in terms of its pace, fluency, and motion. In some respects, we might find frustration in our attempts to ascertain its significance. Is the point simply that the family are *really* enjoying their snack? Yet, the degree of reciprocation that is evoked both through the characters' responses to one another and within their framing draws together some of the underlying themes discussed thus far in relation to *The Royle Family*. The sequence relies almost relentlessly upon the theme of repetition – repeated actions, repeated sounds, repeated positions, repeated sensations, repeated close-ups, repeated camera movements – to the extent that it could almost feel like a redundantly extended portrayal. However, that extension intensifies the centrality of repetition to their relationships with one another and the extent to which it has become a fundamental and defining feature of their interactions. This infuses the exchanges between Barbara, Denise, and Dave as they consciously mirror each other's vocal expressions, but it also extends to the sequence's visual composition, which incorporates both Jim and Anthony within the camera's fluid travelling motion, making them part of the pattern of repetitions that forms between the characters. Indeed, as Jim and Anthony begin and end the travelling dynamic that links the family members together, the show creates a visually replicated relationship between them, which is continued in their bookended positions on separate chairs mirrored either side of the sofa, their enthusiastic consumption of their biscuits, the same slumped posture against the furniture, and even a shared demeanour of mild dissatisfaction (especially when contrasted with the overt satisfaction expressed by Barbara, Denise, and Dave). The aesthetic choices in this sequence, therefore, unite the characters within an overarching structure of repetition.

Repetition, then, is important in *The Royle Family*. As we can see, it runs through the behaviours and attitudes of characters within the show, shaping the relationships that exist between them and, furthermore, becomes a structuring feature within key aspects of aesthetic composition. As I suggested in the opening to this chapter, we might usefully expand this to incorporate a consideration of the relationships that we form as viewers with the show and, particularly in the context of this discussion, the extent to which an investment in the show's dramatic and comedic patterns may involve engaging with those representations that are manifested variously. Repetition becomes the basis for illustrating the characters' affinity to each other, their comfort with one another, and their conscious or unconscious drive to express this through reciprocation, replication, rearticulation, and recapitulation. In this respect, it is entirely possible to view repetition as a positive element within *The Royle Family*, related intrinsically as it is to this family's integral unity and complicity. One of the show's achievements, I would suggest, lies in its ability to articulate this relationship in a manner that is both subdued and understated. With such sustained emphasis placed upon the gentle, mundane rhythms and routines of everyday life, we might risk overlooking the network of relationships that are developed within these instances of repetition (and not least because the interactions themselves are enjoyably humorous).

Finally, we can relate some of these points to the *type* of characters represented in *The Royle Family*. Andy Medhurst provides an account of the show that places class representation at the forefront of discussion, demonstrating persuasively the ways in which preconceptions and even prejudices about class guided journalistic responses to the show, for example (Medhurst 2007, 153–158). Whilst not endeavouring to enter into the precise complexities of such debates here, it is nevertheless important to note that *The Royle Family*'s characters connect with a tradition of working-class representation that might be said to possess a legacy and heritage in British film and television, spanning the twentieth century and into the twenty-first. As a result, the show is presented with options for the way in which it might choose to portray a particular social group. It might, for example, seek to valorise the cultural values that individuals hold (thus offering a well-worn stereotype of the 'noble' working-class, perhaps) or, alternatively, present lifestyle as entrapment: something to be escaped from. This second route would connect with themes found in certain British social realist texts, crystallised in the character of Arthur Seaton (Albert Finney) in *Saturday Night and Sunday Morning* (Karel Reisz 1960), who rebels against his factory-life existence and maintains his famously iconic mantra: 'Don't let the bastards grind you down.'

The Royle Family pursues neither of these routes. There are no rousing speeches about class dignity and strength that might transform characters into mouthpieces for political messaging. Neither is there an assertion that this lifestyle necessitates a desire to escape.[3] (It is the case that Anthony holds somewhat indistinct ambitions to leave home and work in the music industry, but these surely represent the commonplace desires that young people of any background can possess.) Were this second avenue to be pursued, it is entirely possible that repetition might feature as something to be liberated from: as an element that encapsulates the monotonous drudgery of everyday life, for example. Instead, however, *The Royle Family* embraces repetition as a unifying facet within the household, using it to express the bonds that are shared between characters and maintaining it as a central element within relationships of comfort and mutual enjoyment. As a result, the family are represented according to their own group idiosyncrasies, with rituals and routines that are particular to them, rather than as standardised embodiments of a class type. Any reaction on the part of the viewer, therefore, becomes dependent upon the position that *they* adopt in relation to the family (and, as Medhurst's analysis of press reactions to the show demonstrates, certain cultural commentators found it difficult to avoid reverting to sets of assumptions about class and status that they held). In this way, it could be argued that *The Royle Family* in fact avoids making class representation its central focus and, rather, offers a potentially more ambiguous depiction, whereby viewers dictate the kind of relationship they develop with the text. And that relationship, as I have hoped to suggest in this discussion, relies upon and involvement with repetition.

The Trip

In the fifth episode of *The Trip*, Steve (Steve Coogan) and Rob (Rob Brydon) sit together at the bar of The Yorke Arms, Ramsgill.[4] Steve, framed in a medium close-up over Rob's shoulder, is expelling an echoey, raspy noise that seems to emanate from the back of his throat and pass forwards through the fixed oval shape of his open lips. As he makes this sound, he raises a finger in the air, gazing absently in its direction, and rocks his hand back and forth gently, providing a visual evocation of a slight tremor in the tone of his vocal performance. He repeats the noise and gesture a few times as we move to a wider reverse shot of the seated pair.

Rob watches his companion impassively and asks: 'What is that, a sonar?' Steve does not reply but, as we return to the original medium close-up, nods and opens his eyes a little wider in recognition, the flow of his vocal rendition unbroken. Rob joins in with his own attempt at the sonar impression, a little heavier and less delicate than his companion's. With the two now engaged in rhythmic alternation, Steve leans forward and straightens his posture, as though adopting the pose of a teacher. And, indeed, his raised-hand movement becomes a little more emphatic as he times it with his vocal expulsions, accentuating for Rob the technique he is employing and, effectively, tutoring him in the improvement of his own version. They continue the pattern of Rob repeating back Steve's sound as we move between the medium-close up and the wider shot. Steve's efforts do not bear fruit, however, as Rob's rendition becomes less accurate – heavier in the throat, less clearly articulated – the more effort his expends in emulation. Finally, he releases a breath casually from the side of his mouth, no longer attempting the impression and effectively casting it to the side. Steve points to his own mouth, 'No. That's a sonar. You sound like a submarine clearing its throat.' Rob extends the anthropomorphic appraisal, 'I sound like a Scouse submarine,' before making one final, half-hearted attempt. Steve sighs deeply, and a waiter interrupts to take their food orders.

The moment at the bar might justifiably be seen as incidental and, indeed, many scenes within *The Trip* could be described in these terms as the show maintains a modest narrative tone and structure, avoiding accented points of climax. The semi-improvisational production context furthermore allows for sequences like this one to possess a meandering quality, often foregrounding Brydon and Coogan's comic (and dramatic) instincts within the shaping of relatively sparse material. At the same time, and in the context of this book's interests, we might equally note the underlying theme of repetition that guides the pair's interactions: the audial repeating of the sonar sound, Rob's repeating it in an ultimately aborted effort to replicate Steve's impression and the overarching fact that that they attempt to recreate precisely (with contrasting degrees of success) something that already exists: to repeat its qualities. The moment is a slight illustration of the tendency for repetition to become a basis for both performance and competition in *The Trip*. Steven and Rob spend a lot of time repeating the same impressions back to each other across episodes, and those impersonations themselves often contain repetitions of lines and phrases. As they each engage in these acts of replication, a seam of competitiveness emerges, with the pair at times overtly seeking to out-perform one another. Self-evidently, the ability to accurately reproduce the sound of sonar radar is such an esoteric skill that it would struggle to attain any profound importance, yet the men temporarily afford it a centrality within their exchanges, devoting even a focussed intensity to the activity until Rob realises his shortcomings and lets the effort slip. Reflecting on the show's reflexive qualities, Nigel Morris suggests that its 'observational mockumentary aspects stress performance, through impressions – impersonations – that persist to near tedium' (Morris 2015, 424). The impression of the sonar offers an indication of the extent to which impersonation becomes incorporated into Steve and Rob's behaviour almost as an automatic reflex action. The persistence that Morris describes is related to this defining impulse, and tied equally to their willingness to explore or indulge in extremes of repetitive behaviour in the pursuit of honed performance, even for something as apparently trivial as the sonar rendition. Likewise, the 'near tedium' that Morris perceives might conceivably be connected to the pair's consistent desire to undertake another pass at an impersonation without necessarily considering how that might be construed – that, indeed, it might become 'tedious' in a social setting.

In this way, we might understand that Steve and Rob cannot resist – perhaps cannot even avoid – performing to one another, and that their willingness to fall into cycles of repetition as part of that effort represents an urge to perfect an act in each other's eyes. This endeavour is defined by aspects of both intimacy and distance as, on the one hand, the duo collaborates in this repetitive behaviour and, on the other, the nature of their performing means that they are often constructing a barrier between them, averting or delaying directness within the re-evocation of a cast of other human beings through impersonation. In his account of the show, it is possible that Morris over-emphasises the theme of reflexivity to a degree when he asks: 'If these actors can transform themselves so readily, how can viewers tell whether they ever stop acting?' (Ibid). There seems limited value in questioning whether Coogan and Brydon ever stop acting, given that they have created these characters and are playing their parts (although, certainly, a pronounced element of self-reflexivity informs this process in *The Trip*), meaning that we would never satisfactorily arrive at an answer. Indeed, conflating the personas of actors and characters too strongly may risk overlooking or misrepresenting Coogan and Brydon's achievements *as* actors. However, we can legitimately ask whether the characters, Steve and Rob, ever stop acting and, furthermore, what the persistent return to and recapitulation of that activity might represent. There is protection, no doubt, in the partial adoption of different personas and it is perhaps appropriate to equate this with an emotional insecurity that both men experience to different degrees, and which is manifested in a drive to intersperse conversations with deviating vignettes that reinforce the security of mediated role-play. As these impressions become imbued with aspects of repetition, it perhaps illustrates Steve and Rob's particular dedication to not only the perfection of impressions for each other but also their determination to maintain certain barriers between them. It is ironic, therefore, that they should engage closely in spirals of wordplay and vocal rearticulation together but, in doing so, express a shared but unspoken need to preserve distance in their relationship, which they achieve by adopting temporarily the style and manner of other personas.

The repeating patterns of impersonation also give rise to bursts of creative improvisation, as both Steve and Rob demonstrate their comedic skills in expanding source material to construct fresh humorous scenarios that might involve incongruous or surreal associations. As they sit at the bar in this scene, Steve raises the subject of the ABBA song 'The Winner Takes It All,' suggesting that 'the reason that song has so much pain is because he wrote the words for her to sing about their breakup, but he wrote the lyrics from her point of view.' It is notable, perhaps, that Steve should alight upon this apocryphal example, given that it involves an individual using their art to displace emotion, rather than confront it directly, which represents a heightened version of what both he and Rob engage in through their repeated reversion to competitive impressions in *The Trip*. (We might also note that Steve again adopts the role of teacher, imparting knowledge in a similar fashion to his sonar radio instruction, thus attaining authority in the pair's competitive relationship, certainly, but also exhibiting an enduring commitment to understanding the world through its obscure facets.) He doesn't let his contemplation of the song rest, however, and instead begins to sing lines from it in a gentle tone and with a tenderness that is inherently funny due to the incongruity of a middle-aged man sitting at a bar softly reciting ABBA lyrics. The style of delivery is also in keeping with the way both Steve and Rob engage through impressions. They are shot from the side as they face each other in mirrored positions on the bar stools, in a composition that accentuates the directness and closeness of Steve's singing to Rob.

Figure 4.3 The Trip.

Yet, of course, he is performing as ABBA lead vocalist Agnetha Fältskog singing lyrics written by Benny Anderson and Björn Ulvaeus, a relationship that he has further complicated through the backstory of Ulvaeus and Fältskog's separation and its impact upon the tone and content of the words. His performance, therefore, encapsulates themes of intimacy and distance that often underscore the relationship between Steve and Rob, possessing a markedly direct intensity but, at the same time, defined by elements of separation and detachment.

Characteristically, Rob joins in with Steve's rendition but then breaks off to comment that Ulvaeus is being 'a bit presumptuous' in suggesting through his lyrics that Fältskog has no self-confidence (a line they have just sung together). This prompts him to launch into his own impression of Fältskog insisting that she does have self-confidence, she is just 'sad about the break-up.' Again, Rob's rotating of the simple term 'self-confidence' illustrates his capacity, shared with Steve, to revisit minute, even trivial, details as part of a creative effort to discover extra depths of meaning and, often, additional comic potential. We might recognise that we are being shown glimpses of a process here, very familiar to both Brydon and Coogan, whereby comedians revolve and fixate upon minutiae to tease out extra meanings that might otherwise be missed but, ultimately, resonate with audiences. We can also appreciate that, although the show continues to emphasise Steve and Rob's union within shots like the side-on view and another from a right-hand angle that frames their pairing in an otherwise deserted bar, Rob's interjection is marking out a deviation in the conversation that runs against notions of a shared closeness between the two and constructs a further potential barrier as he briefly adopts the persona of Fältskog.

A sharp cut takes us to the kitchen of the Yorke Arms as Steve and Rob's starters are called by the head chef. A trio of shots depicts two souffles being poured, tapped, and placed into a stove-top *bain marie*. This interlude has a clear functional purpose, reminding us of the location and the characters' reasons for being there (Steve has been commissioned to write a series of restaurant reviews for the *Observer* newspaper). At the same time, however, the relatively blunt edit that takes us to the kitchen offers a forceful allusion to the fact that these two men are part of and, indeed, reliant upon, a wider pattern of repetition: repetitive labour in a workplace. The banging of the souffles on the work surface to remove pockets of air in the mixture provides an almost playfully metaphoric and unceremonious deflation of the celebrity ego that Steve and Rob each possess in different ways, reframing their identities as anonymous customers within a repeating cycle of culinary preparation. They are no different, in this respect, to the customers who came yesterday or those who will come tomorrow and, indeed, in this world they are simply the 'one souffle, one tuna,' read out by the head chef.

We cut back to the bar as Steve and Rob continue to sing a verse from 'The Winner Takes It All.' They are both affecting broad Swedish accents of sorts (ABBA's home nation being Sweden) but Steve picks up Rob on specificity in the pronunciation of 'hurting,' suggesting that Fältskog says 'hurding' in her accent. Rob repeats this back a few times before cautioning Steve against making her sound like 'the chef from the Muppets,' following this with a singsong 'hirdy, birdy, girdy.' Steve returns this critique when Rob overemphasises some of his consonant sounds in another recital of the verse, telling him that he sounds like 'the Nazi from *Inglourious Basterds* [Quentin Tarantino, 2009]' and accompanying this with a short rendition of a scene from that film. Rob, however, has restarted the verse again in a much more pronounced German accent, which Steve initially joins in with but then attempts to withdraw from by looking down and saying 'erm ... .' By now, though, the transition in accents has led Rob into a favourite impression of a Bond villain, and then finally his Roger Moore. At this point, Steve's demeanour is much more passive and he is no longer engaged with the game of improvised impersonation. He concludes by saying, in a subdued tone, 'I find the song quite moving' and raises his hand lightly in a gesture of placid resignation.

Steve's final remark indicates a degree of dissatisfaction with the way in which his remark about the ABBA song has instigated yet another cycle of impromptu imitations. Yet, he has been a participant in this process and, consequently, it is perhaps more accurate to suggest that he voices frustration at being unable to restrain the impulses that drive many of his and Rob's interactions: their tendency to fall into repetitions of favourite impressions and their penchant for improvised play. The dramatic setup of *The Trip* dictates straightforwardly that the two characters are regularly framed in a position of physical mirroring – most often at restaurant tables, but also in instances like this bar scene. This arrangement gives emphasis to the fact that they are regularly repeating back to one another types of behaviour and even specific impressions and lines of dialogue, to the extent that they not only physically mirror one another but also echo each other in their vocal delivery. This results in a cyclical pattern of exchange and interaction, whereby forward momentum is often curtailed as they allow themselves (or, indeed, encourage each other) to get pulled back into the recital of familiar material. Steve's point about the pain inherent in the lyrics to 'The Winner Takes It All' is therefore unlikely to find development within their conversation, hence his mild irritation at the end of the scene. Instead, even slight details like the word 'hurting' are lingered upon and evaluated, placing an emphasis upon form over content or, more accurately, surface over depth. Furthermore, developing an understanding of pain in the lyrics of a pop song might equally involve Steve and Rob articulating their own understanding of that pain, and developing an understanding of human emotion together. This does not seem a path they are equipped to take and, instead, their relationship is reliant upon a type of mediated closeness, ensuring that they can spend hours together but on the unspoken condition that they regularly place certain performative barriers around themselves. The repetition of the same impressions offers a reassertion of this agreement, just as the existence of a competitive instinct within their interactions justifies the perpetual return by reframing it as a form of (professional) refinement.

For Steve and Rob, then, each repetition reinforces the nature of their relationship. This endures in the final episode, when they perform 'The Winner Takes It All' once more. Driving from their final destination, Rob raises the dilemma that Steve faces over joining his girlfriend in America or not. After some hesitative responses, Steve says he doesn't want to talk about it, which prompts Rob to say 'You don't want to talk about things you've gone through?' which in turn leads to Steve responding with 'No ... Though it's hurting me ...' and then they are both reciting directly from the song: 'Now it's history ...' before singing verses together. This rendition bears a relationship to the earlier instance in the bar, as they slip in and out of loose Swedish accents and correct each other's misquotations but, gazes fixed out beyond the glass of the windscreen and positioned comfortably side-by-side in the car interior, the two men appear more invested in the straightforward performance of the song rather than the earlier, self-conscious, Agnetha-mediated-through-Bjorn-mediated-through-Agnetha version. The sequence is shot from a camera rigged to the front of the vehicle, which frames either Coogan or Brydon, or from a back seat position providing a reverse shot of each. This arrangement isolates each character and affords them their own space inside the vehicle: there is no two-shot and only an exterior long-shot of the vehicle containing both men.

Figure 4.4 The Trip.

Figure 4.5 The Trip.

This form of visual compartmentalisation complements a sense of ease that underscores their performance of the song now. Within their respective zones, they do not express the same direct competitiveness and, indeed, they now correct one another in a collaborative effort, conceding their own mistakes genially. It is as though, for a few short moments, these men have discovered an environment in which intimacy and distance – two guiding elements in their relationship – can co-exist and find balance, which in turn reshapes their behaviour. This zonal separation extends to moments when each character becomes temporarily absorbed in the song, their respective gaze settling absently on the road in front as they experience aspects of the reflection and regret inherent in the song's lyrics.

There is a shift in mood, however, when they reach the climax of their rendition. The pace and force of their singing have been building up to this point and, then, they finish with four exuberant repetitions of the line 'The Winner Takes It All,' their voices rising fervently and, indeed, Steven ending on an ambitious high-note. Their return to the song, therefore, culminates in a moment of joyful release, which draws the meaning away from the sadness that Steve had identified in the earlier bar scene. At the same time, their recital has also incorporated elements of quieter introspection, providing a pattern of fluctuating contrasts in its duration. The return to 'The Winner Takes It All' has provided an opportunity to reshape its meanings and effects, offering a chance for the two men to take another pass at understanding its significance for them. This has, however, revealed the ambiguous impact it has upon them, to the extent that they engage with it both meditatively and joyfully without necessarily understanding their reactions. This impulsive response contrasts with Steve's earlier attempt to attach a specific quality to the song and, furthermore, an exact reason for that quality (the separation of the two band members as a context). We can extend this to propose that their discovery of its ambiguous resonances connects with an ambiguity that is fundamental to their friendship. The hesitation between intimacy and distance, which finds a point of equilibrium within this car interior at this moment, carries with it a resistance to settle and be defined. Revisiting 'The Winner Takes It All' takes its place in a pattern of incessant repetitions that Steve and Rob construct, but it also allows them to rediscover a quality in their friendship. In having yet another attempt at performing the ABBA song, they are taking another pass at the idea of being together and, perhaps unexpectedly, arrive at a version of companionship that can provide momentary comfort and pleasure. The jubilant climax of the song, which represents an imaginative reshaping of its form, therefore represents a celebration of their idiosyncratic bond. Repetition, so central to their behaviour and interactions throughout *The Trip*, has provided this.

Notes

1 This is certainly the case for the first two seasons of *Royle Family*, but it is worth noting that later episodes did move the action beyond the walls of the Royles' home, to locations such as a caravan park and Dave and Denise's house.
2 Cash and Aherne's awareness deriving from the fact that they, of course, are the creators of this comedy drama.
3 In this respect, the song that plays over the show's opening credits, Oasis' 'Half the World Away' might actually be read as somewhat incongruous, describing, as it does, a fervent and escalating desire to escape.
4 In *The Trip*, Steve Coogan and Rob Brydon play characters, based loosely on their own personas, called Steve Coogan and Rob Brydon. This presents certain challenges in terms of differentiating between actors and characters. In an article on the show, Michael Allen and Janet McCabe distinguish the characters by calling them 'Coogan' and 'Brydon' (Allen and McCabe 2012, 151). This is a practical measure, certainly, but it also derives from an understanding of the characters as 'media constructs' and 'artifices' (Ibid). Within this chapter, I am invested more in the idea of these characters as real people that exist within a fictional world. Consequently, I refer to the characters as Steve and Rob, and the actors as Coogan and Brydon (denoting their professional ownership of the screen depictions they create).

5   Repetition and Resurrection

The various forms of television content can often involve patterns of repetition and, indeed, this can constitute a prominent structuring element. We might think of soap operas, for example, which have an exceptionally regular broadcast schedule and revolve around the same locations, events, and characters. These characters necessarily possess firmly defined traits and, as a consequence, are predisposed to repeating the same kinds of behaviours over and over again, meaning that progression and growth are curtailed to an extent within cycles of perpetual recapitulation. Or we might turn to long-running detective dramas, in which a sleuthing amateur or professional detective will encounter murder after murder at a rate that surely exceeds any real homicide statistics. Variation comes, of course, in the fact that each case possesses its own motives and traits but, nevertheless, these shows conform to an overarching structure of repetition and return.

A tension can occur when the continuity of these repeating forms becomes compromised by certain influencing production contexts. While a format can hypothetically continue in perpetuity, for example, actors cannot. For soap operas, this dilemma is resolved within large and various casts that allow individuals to depart without bringing the show to an end or even causing profound disruption. For detective dramas, there is a greater dilemma when the show has centred itself around a singular or titular character, such as Jessica Fletcher (Angela Lansbury) in *Murder, She Wrote* (CBS 1984–1996) or Lieutenant Columbo (Peter Falk) in *Columbo* (NBC 1968–1978; ABC 1989–2003). These shows arguably could not and, indeed, did not endure after the departure of star actors whose identities were so deeply embedded in their identity and texture. Other creative directions can be explored: *Inspector Morse* (ITV 1987–2000) could not feasibly continue after the death of main actor John Thaw, so other shows were launched that explored related aspects of that character's story. *Lewis* (ITV 2006–2015) continued the narrative by focussing on

DOI: 10.4324/9781003265283-6

Morse's erstwhile sidekick and *Endeavour* (ITV 2012-) moved in the opposite direction, offering a prequel to *Inspector Morse* by depicting the titular character's earlier life. These last three examples are significant inasmuch as they offer an indication of television's almost instinctive drive, governed by commercial imperatives and/or creative desire, to continue successful shows and formats: to revisit them and recapture that success. It is probably accurate to say that commercial imperatives enjoy the greater priority over creative desire, as evidenced by the sometimes apparently brutal way in which shows are discontinued when they are deemed to have exhausted their potential for future success.

Repetition, therefore, can become a strong guiding feature in the broader television landscape as shows offer a recapitulation of their own characteristics even as they move forward with new episodes and series. This chapter will consider the effects of this upon the thematic and aesthetic composition of particular shows – how an awareness of a repeating structure is acknowledged and incorporated into narrative form and presentational style, for example. I would contend that many long-running shows with repetition as a structuring feature can demonstrate a kind of self-awareness in different ways and to varying degrees. Characters in soap operas might become frustrated when friends or family slip yet again into repeated patterns of behaviour (especially those that are self-destructive or antisocial) and the screen detective may express a degree of weariness when yet another murder case offers an illustration of the fallible and tragic human condition. In this sense, my chosen examples are not entirely exceptional. However, I am interested in the extent to which they are aware, and in turn make us aware, of the idea that repetition can also be resurrection. This may mean straightforwardly the resurrection of a format or narrative structure, but it can also become more focussed, involving the resurrection of a character, for example, which in turn provides opportunities to reflect upon and explore what that kind of process might involve and the nature of its impacts.

Robin of Sherwood

In its second season, the makers of *Robin of Sherwood* (ITV 1984–1986) were faced with a dilemma when the actor playing Robin, Michael Praed, announced that he was leaving to pursue a career in the United States. Series creator Richard Carpenter arrived at a solution by drawing upon an Elizabethan version of the Robin Hood myth that allowed for an entirely different character to take on the persona of the hero (Chapman 2015, 162). Consequently, Jason Connery's Robert of Huntingdon replaced Praed's Robin of Locksley.

The option Carpenter pursued is perhaps representative of a particular fluidity offered by the Robin Hood legend and, indeed, Thomas Leitch has noted that 'no definitive articulation of the myth can be identified' on screen (Leitch 2008, 22), and that the famous Allan Dwan film version of 1922, starring Douglas Fairbanks, includes Robert of Huntingdon rather than Robin of Locksley 'as he should have been called' (Ibid, 21). Additionally, Carpenter had introduced a mystical quality to his version of the Robin Hood story (Chapman, 153), with the enigmatic character of Herne the Hunter (John Abineri) possessing a magical link to the hero. This element provides an opportunity for continuity between incumbents, as the spiritual connection is retained in any new configuration, and this is indeed employed in scenes when Herne effectively inducts Huntingdon into the role.

In the show, Locksley is killed by the Sheriff of Nottingham's (Nicholas Grace) soldiers (season two, episode seven). He has been trapped on a rocky hill with two other characters, Marian (Judi Trott) and Much (Peter Llewellyn Williams), but they escape, leaving Locksley to face the small army alone. The lighting has been naturalistic up to this point but, with the Sheriff giving the order to attack, we cut to a long shot of Locksley standing at the summit in silhouette with the sun behind him, bow drawn, and a red filter has been placed on the lens. This changes not only the visual representation of the character but also the mood of the scene, imbuing it with a mystical quality and enhancing the iconography of Robin Hood. As the sheriff orders his men forward, Locksley fires arrows at them, killing individual soldiers as they advance. The sheriff and his forces are still depicted in the natural light but, as we return to Locksley in a repeat of the long shot and then a tighter medium-long shot, he is again framed in the red-filtered light. A distinction is thus established between the ordinariness of one setting and the extraordinariness of another, as though Locksley exists in a realm distinct from the real world and, therefore, seemingly elevated above the normal conventions of human life. The Sheriff, realising that his men are being picked off, has ordered a temporary retreat but, finally, Locksley reaches his final arrow, casts his quiver away, and walks slowly along the ridge in medium shot. We cut back to the assembled soldiers moving back tentatively again as he performs this action, which represents a reasonable precaution but also illustrates the power that he exerts in this sequence, whereby even his relatively small movements provoke mass action. In medium close-up, Locksley directs his arrow skywards, looks down, and loosens it. We cut to a long shot of him, standing on the rocky summit, bow raised, silhouetted against the sun once more.

Figure 5.1 Robin of Sherwood.

Both shots retain the red filter, enhancing a moment of symbolic relinquishment. The soldiers watch the arrow soar over their heads, and then they advance. We cut back to a close-up of Locksley as he expresses a slight smile of acknowledgement and nods his head in the direction of the Sheriff (whose uncertain response is captured in reverse-shot) before he walks away in medium-long shot. A troop of crossbow archers appear and he turns away from them, walks a few steps, before pausing and finally snapping his bow in two. The music, which has been building in tension, ends abruptly on this action, creating a moment of synthesis between character and aesthetic depiction. In the silence that follows, the Sheriff calls out 'Shoot!' and the archers unleash their arrows in Locksley's direction. We cut back to the Sheriff saying 'At last,' and then the screen fades to black as his men advance in Locksley's direction.

The aesthetic portrayal of Locksley's final moments enhances and elevates the significance of the scene. His visual depiction in the red-filtered light, and within a series of framing choices that accentuate his iconic imagery, creates a marked distinction not only between him and the amassed army but also between this man and ordinary human life. The character is made special within this representation, reinforcing his centrality within the show's narrative, and connecting Locksley with an overarching enigmatic mysticism. (Additionally, in the broader production context, Praed is afforded a climactic final scene as the creative decisions enrich and commemorate his departure.) The shots of the silhouetted Locksley in that strange supernatural light maintain a mysterious quality that has surrounded his character throughout the two seasons, setting him within but inherently apart from his comrades and presenting him as almost magically undefeatable – hence the Sheriff's emphatic relief in this sequence's conclusion. The phrase 'hooded man' is referenced in the *Robin of Sherwood*'s theme song, and this notion is retained within the show, making its central character iconic but also inscrutable. A point of continuity is established, therefore, in Huntingdon's introduction as the next 'Robin' within the episode: he remains hooded in every scene as his identity is withheld. Indeed, having loosened his own arrow in tribute to Locksley at a woodland ceremony held by the band of followers, the camera zooms in slightly on Huntingdon standing, bow in hand and hooded. The image is frozen and held as the end credits roll over it, imprinting the notion that a new hero, possessing the appropriate iconic traits, has emerged.[1]

With this in mind, we can see that the opening of the first episode of season three plots a different direction. We re-join the memorial to Locksley (interspersed with additional recaps from the last season) and Huntingdon fires his arrow. Immediately afterwards, however, he turns and walks away from the scene, ignoring the cries of the assembled group for him to return and reveal himself.

Figure 5.2 Robin of Sherwood.

A tracking shot moves with him as he removes his hood and continues his retreat, and then we are presented with a series of intercuts between Huntingdon as he makes his way through the forest and Herne, standing still on higher ground, wearing a deer's head as mists swirl around him. The pair conduct a kind of psychic dispute (communicating only in thoughts) as Huntingdon expresses his strong reluctance to become Robin Hood and Herne insists that he take on the role. It ends with Huntingdon saying 'Farewell, Herne' and holding up his bow and arrow before letting them drop to the ground, relinquishing the duty they symbolise. Herne's voice is heard, saying 'You are the hooded man' but this contradicts the image of Huntingdon with his hood removed, abandoning the title. We might note that the depiction of Huntingdon against Herne marks a reversal of the way Locksley was represented in his final moments. There, Locksley was the mystical figure, occupying the higher ground and rendered supernatural against the soldiers' ordinariness: here, Herne is placed in the enigmatic, elevated position and Huntingdon is rendered ordinary – a position that he actually seeks.

Although Huntingdon's succession as Robin Hood is never properly in doubt (this scene is followed immediately by a title sequence depicting him very definitely in the role, for example), the nature of this episode's opening is nevertheless significant. It dramatises the burden of heroism by emphasising it as a human choice and, furthermore, exploring the continuing duty of being 'Robin Hood' as it passes from one individual to another. In doing so, the show places at stake the notion of a repeating heroic narrative continuing, as the central character confronts the option of taking it up and carrying on, or walking away from it. This kind of repetitive burden, I would suggest, can be related to another work of fiction, 'The Myth of Sisyphus.' The myth is relatively familiar. Having cheated death twice and having, at one stage, put an end to death itself, Sisyphus is condemned by the Gods to forever push a rock to the top of a summit, only to see it roll down again and begin the effort once more. Sisyphus' act is endlessly cyclical, and hence the word "Sisyphean" has become a kind of metonym in contemporary culture for an apparently ever-repeating task. Indeed, the ubiquity and straightforwardness of the term may create an obstacle to the myth of Sisyphus being considered in any great detail: it has general relevance to a relatable condition and, as a consequence, we may feel that we already understand and appreciate any significance it holds. Certainly, the myth of Sisyphus has not inspired the same complex range of references that the myths of Odysseus or Heracles have, for example. There may be good reasons for this. Unlike those myths, there is no quest, no end, and no obvious heroism to Sisyphus' story. As a narrative, it is especially limited and presents a challenge to anyone seeking a meaningful resolution. It is perhaps these qualities that leads Richard Taylor to suggest that, in the myth:

We have the picture of meaninglessness, pointless toil, of a meaningless existence that is absolutely *never* redeemed. It is not even redeemed by a death that, if it were to accomplish nothing more, would at least bring this idiotic cycle to a close [...]. Nothing comes of it, nothing at all.

(Taylor 2000, 320 [emphasis in original])

Aspects of this reading might be seen to encapsulate Huntingdon's thoughts on the specific duty he is presented with: that it would never find redemption and could constitute 'pointless toil.' Indeed, we can extend it further if we consider certain qualities of the continuing television title, which can embody this kind of incessant return without resolution as part of commercial and creative impulses to carry on and, indeed, re-tread familiar ground. In exploring Huntingdon's reservations, therefore, *Robin of Sherwood* might be seen to contemplate its own status and qualities, pausing for a moment to question, albeit temporarily, what is at stake in restarting the cycle with a new player and, as a consequence, drawing our attention to its practical apparatus *as* a television show. Moving wider still, we can place the moment within the much larger spread of the Robin Hood myth, which has spanned centuries and incorporated many kinds of variations in its retelling (Leitch, 21). This is a grand and ever-expanding narrative that, through an extended process of continual recapitulation, has never found resolution. From a certain perspective, therefore, it might well conform to some of the characteristics that Taylor suggests to be present in the myth of Sisyphus.

It is apparent that, in Taylor's reading of the Sisyphus myth, the central characteristic of perpetual return becomes, in itself, an act devoid of meaningful purpose and worth. The discussion might end there (providing the kind of resolution a Sisyphean narrative cannot) if we did not attend to Albert Camus' alternative earlier reading of Sisyphus, which counters implicitly some of the claims Taylor wishes to make and, as a consequence, provides us with a possible means of finding value in the repetitive structures that *Robin of Sherwood* draws attention to. Camus sees Sisyphus as the archetype of the absurd hero, a man who is conscious of his plight, of his misery, and of his tragedy and yet continues without appeal to unseen Gods, and without the release of death. In achieving this aim, Camus attempts to see Sisyphus not simply as a straightforwardly symbolic mythical figure but as a physical and psychological reality. He begins with the physical:

As for this myth, one sees merely the whole effort of a body straining to raise the huge stone, to roll it and push it up a slope a hundred times over; one sees the face screwed up, the cheek tight against the stone, the shoulder bracing the clay-covered mass, the foot wedging it, the fresh start with arms outstretched, the wholly human security of two earth-clotted hands.

(Camus [1955] 2005, 116)

What should strike us immediately from this passage is the way in which Camus engages sincerely with the act that Sisyphus finds himself performing again and again. Where most accounts of Sisyphus' life quite understandably *end* with his eternal punishment (his fate), Camus takes this as a starting point, imagining what that punishment might look like and, crucially, how it might feel. And, rather than seeing Sisyphus' existence as only the epitome of meaningless repetition, Camus goes on to consider what meaning could be found in such an existence. As a way of approaching those questions, he concerns himself with the moment at which the rock has rolled back yet again, and Sisyphus must descend to retrieve it. Camus says that:

> It is during that return, that pause, that Sisyphus interests me. A face that toils so close to stones is already stone itself! I see that man going back with a heavy yet measured step towards the torment of which he will never know the end. That hour like a breathing-space which returns as surely as his suffering, that is the hour of consciousness. At each of those moments when he leaves the heights and gradually sinks towards the lairs of the gods, he is superior to his fate. He is stronger than his rock.
>
> (Camus, 117)

Camus finds an unlikely nobility and honour in the myth of Sisyphus that Taylor's account can never accommodate. For Camus, it is the moment of descent once the stone has rolled back down that provides the greatest emphasis of Sisyphus' strength and resolve. Taylor interprets this moment as Sisyphus' life at its most meaningless yet, in Camus' account, that same character finds his peak of moral determination at the very point when he makes yet another physical descent.

If this introduces a more optimistic and even heroic interpretation of Sisyphus' fate, it is also true that Camus regards the myth as tragic precisely because the hero is *conscious* of his burden. Indeed, the 'hour of consciousness' provides Sisyphus with arguably his greatest test, when the hopeless repetition of his labour stretches out before him. This, we might contend, is precisely the moment that *Robin of Sherwood* chooses to dramatise onscreen as Huntingdon demonstrates his awareness of the burden that he is being asked to carry as both heroic and tragic, and greets it initially with resistance. Here, he is Sisyphus at the foot of the mountain, in the 'breathing-space' that Camus describes. Like Camus' perception of Sisyphus, we are asked to consider Huntingdon as a corporeal entity, unhooded, ordinary, and devoid of any mystical associations, his moment of hesitancy registering as the human instinct of a real person. Yet, the hesitancy reaches out into broader contexts to attain symbolic weight, as his decision becomes bound to the cyclical continuation of the show and, beyond that, the further recapitulation of the Robin Hood myth itself. Consequently, *Robin of Sherwood* reveals its consciousness of the various elements that are balanced within the moment, and what is at stake in Huntingdon's deciding whether or not to re-engage with a pattern of perpetual return. And yet, like Sisyphus, he is fated to continue. Herne's words are founded upon an insistence that he is destined to continue the legacy ('You're Herne's son, you must lead them': 'You were chosen'), and, significantly, the sequence ends with him stating: 'You will return. You must.'

It is perhaps inevitable, then, that Huntingdon should eventually take on the mantle of Robin Hood and embrace the burden that it represents (thus, in turn, resurrecting the show's intrinsic format as well as the heroic myth itself). It is notable that this process is extended across the first two episodes of the third season and that it is depicted as a struggle: Huntingdon has to persuade Locksley's comrades to join with him and even has to fight them in turn as he endeavours to earn their trust and respect. As a result, the show commits itself to the hardships of the role that Huntingdon reinstates, thus forming a connection with notions of Sisyphean toil as arduous and unforgiving. As the narrative restarts with a new incumbent, so the whole fabric of the world must be restored: the rock must be returned to the summit. Indeed, we might presume that a new leader could face the same task if Huntingdon were to fall, according to the pattern the show has now established. There is a commitment, therefore, to perpetual continuation and reiteration, rather than progress toward finality and resolution. The cancelling of *Robin of Sherwood* after this third season in fact reinforces this idea, denying narrative closure and conveying a sense of the cyclical process carrying on in perpetuity, even though we will not see it. Cancellation can, for obvious reasons, be regarded as an especially abrupt ending for any television show but, in the case of *Robin of Sherwood*, we can see that it instead, and perhaps ironically, complements notions of a Sisyphean continuity extending ceaselessly into the future. Indeed, the character of Robin Hood does not end with this show by any means, and the wider continuity extends to include major feature films like *Robin Hood: Prince of Thieves* (Kevin Reynolds 1991) and *Robin Hood* (Ridley Scott 2010), as well as the BBC television series *Robin Hood* (2006–2009). As a result, the broader cycle of perpetual repetition continues across media texts, newly resurrecting the mythical character with every retelling.

Doctor Who

Robin of Sherwood was not, of course, the first show to face the issue of replacing its main actor, with the archetypal case in British television being *Doctor Who* (BBC 1963–1989; 2005-). Due to the deteriorating health of lead William Hartnell, the role was recast in 1966 and, because the Doctor is an extra-terrestrial being, the producers arrived at the novel idea that he or she can change the bodily form, thus providing a narrative logic for the same character to be played by a new actor, Patrick Troughton. Later termed 'regeneration,' this process of re-casting has become a major component of the show's narrative structure and its expanding character mythology. In turn, the moment of regeneration has enjoyed an increasing degree of dramatic emphasis, particularly during the post-2005 rebooted or 'new' era, and a related self-consciousness within the show that extends the levels I suggested were at play in the *Robin of Sherwood* example. We might observe a degree of reflection regarding the re-casting of a new actor so that the Doctor's farewell becomes intermingled with the performer's, and likewise a linking together of the character's regeneration and the show's continuity – carrying on with a new face – as well as the wider, overarching mythology of the Doctor – adding yet more layers of detail and complexity through the introduction of a new inhabitant to the role. However, the moment of regeneration can also mark a transition between showrunners, from Russell T Davies to Steven Moffat to Chris Chibnall in the 'new' era, for example, and so the nature of its depiction might also be equated to their final act in the role (or, indeed, a final flourish).[2]

The longevity of the show and its self-consciousness regarding the regeneration process creates a relationship with notions of a Sisyphean narrative, as we find not only the character but also related aspects of the production poised at the point of continuity. Furthermore, an audio-visual emphasis is placed upon the decision to persevere in an undertaking that provides no resolution, and in which any accomplishment is accompanied by a perpetual return. Just before his own regeneration, in a 2017 Christmas episode 'Twice Upon a Time,' the twelfth Doctor (Peter Capaldi) delivers a set of reflections that are not dissimilar in tone to Huntingdon's response to the prospect of becoming Robin Hood. The Doctor is talking to glass avatars that have taken the form of his deceased companions, Bill (Pearl Mackie) and Nardole (Matt Lucas), on a deserted First World War battlefield. The episode has involved the question of whether this Doctor (and, indeed, the First Doctor (David Bradley), whom he encounters) will regenerate at all. Nardole offers a suggestion: 'Don't die. Because if you do, I think everyone in the universe might just go cold.' The Doctor replies: 'Can't I ever have peace? Can't I rest?' For the second of these questions, he is framed in an extreme close-up that accentuates the potent sense of strain and weariness that Capaldi brings to the role, certainly in this final season.

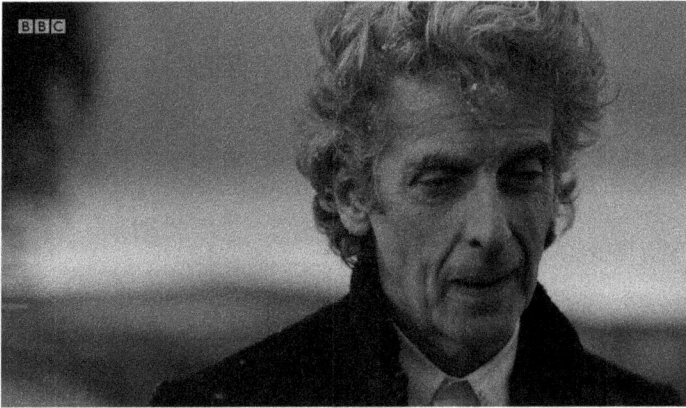

Figure 5.3 Doctor Who.

Letting his gaze drop, he tautens his features by half-closing his eyes and tightening his lips slightly, causing a series of deep-set lines and contours to form across his face as he speaks. The image might well evoke Camus' description of Sisyphus, 'a face that toils so close to stones is already stone itself,' as Capaldi's performance underscores the physicality of the burden that his character experiences, aligning with the psychological weight his words encapsulate, and captured in the show's aesthetic composition. In this respect, it is appropriate that the Doctor should associate death with 'peace' and 'rest,' suggesting that it offers the only respite from apparently eternal toil. Capaldi conveys the impression of a character that has done this for a very long time and is worn out by the effort.

This theme is picked up in the Doctor's response to the avatar-companion's suggestion that they understand his situation:

> No. No you don't. You're not even really here. You're just memories, held in glass. Do you know how many of you I could fill? I would shatter you. My testimony would shatter all of you. A life this long, do you understand what it is? It's a battlefield, like this one. And it's empty, because everyone else has fallen. Thank you, thank both for everything that you were to me. What happens now, where I go, now, has to be alone.

The speech references the fact that these glass avatars are living archives for human memories, and it concludes with the Doctor embracing these entities, as though instinct finally draws him to even these constructed versions of his old friends. Until that point, the framing pattern has depicted Bill and Nardole in a two-shot and the Doctor in a series of close-ups, creating a sense of his isolation within this sequence and, more broadly within the span of existence that he describes. And these close-ups continue the interrogation of his features, picking out the points of contemplation and resignation that are contained within Capaldi's portrayal and focussing again on the physical manifestations of these thoughts. Again, we might consider that we are presented with a vision of Sisyphus here, discovering a moment of pause before resuming his task, Camus' 'breathing space.' The enigmatic final line raises the ambiguous suggestion that the Doctor may follow his instincts and withdraw, breaking the cycle of repetition and thus relinquishing his Sisyphean affliction forever through death. Indeed, he concludes this scene by saying 'Time to leave the battlefield' and, when he enters his phone-box time machine (the TARDIS), he makes yet more specific reference to the recapitulating nature of his life's duty: 'Oh, there it is. Silly old universe. The more I save it, the more it needs saving. It's a treadmill.' Yet, the phrase 'silly old universe' perhaps hints at a subtle change in perspective, alluding to a degree of affection the character feels in his predicament and, likewise, the acknowledgement of 'the more I save it …' may suggest a burgeoning intention to *continue* the rotation of rescues even if, like a 'treadmill,' it never completes. Hence the line, soon after: 'Well, I suppose one more lifetime won't kill anyone. Well, except me.' And so, in Sisyphean terms, the journey back to the summit has resumed, undertaken with the 'heavy yet measured step towards the torment of which he will never know the end' that Camus describes.

Perhaps this is the defining characteristic of the Doctor's heroism: the unwavering return to the unending duty as Universal saviour. In Camus' terms, to prove, time and again, that he is 'stronger than his rock.' However, *Doctor Who* offers further allusions to Camus' reading of Sisyphus when, with regeneration complete, the next Doctor (Jodie Whittaker) utters her first words with an exuberant grin: 'Oh, brilliant!'

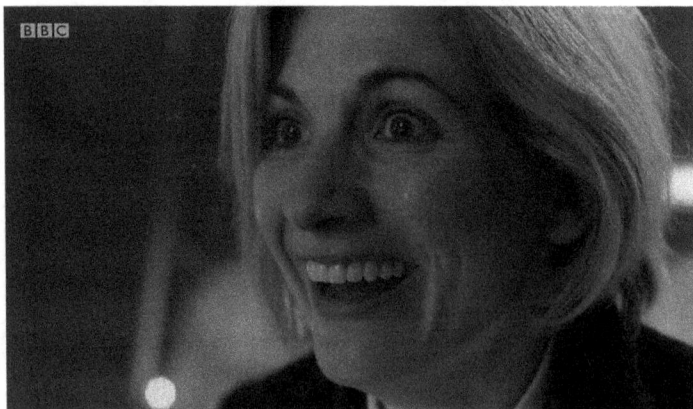

Figure 5.4 Doctor Who.

This response is important, as it illustrates not only the character's willingness to resume her burden but also, unequivocally, her joy in doing so. Camus concludes his reading of Sisyphus with the contention: 'The struggle itself towards the heights is enough to fill a man's heart. One must imagine Sisyphus happy' (Camus, 119), and *Doctor Who* goes a step further to provide an emphatic visual depiction of that happiness as it is experienced by its own Sisyphean hero once the unending journey has recommenced. The expression of delight might also be connected to the fact that, with Whittaker's casting, the Doctor was finally being depicted as a woman for the first time. Again, we might relate this duality of meaning to the show's self-referentiality, and the extent to which it is able to reflect and comment upon features of its production context within the same moment.

Further aspects of self-reference exist in Whittaker's introduction, however. Immediately after her regeneration, the musical theme of the tenth Doctor (David Tennant) can be heard on the soundtrack and this coincides with a slow-motion close-up of a ring falling from her finger onto the floor of the TARDIS. This visual detail recalls a moment from the eleventh Doctor's (Matt Smith) regeneration when he unfastens his bowtie and lets it fall to the floor of the TARDIS in a gesture of relinquishment. In one sense, this combination of motifs from the tenth and eleventh Doctors might provide a straightforward reminder that the process of regeneration has a history, and that a number of incarnations have preceded this current one.[3] Yet, within that allusion, we might also recall the nature of the transition between those two earlier Doctors. David Tennant's tenth Doctor is afforded an especially long goodbye in a sequence that occupies over twenty minutes at the end of another Christmas special, *The End of Time* (2010). Indeed, this is the second part of two special episodes broadcast over the Christmas period, and the subject of his departure has occupied both predominantly (as well as extending into earlier special episodes). As a result, his regeneration is afforded not only a narrative definition but also emotional significance. The extended farewell might be seen to begin at the point where having repelled the twin threats to Earth from the Master (John Simm) and a consortium of Time Lords headed by Rassilon (Timothy Dalton), the Doctor is visibly moved to find that he is still alive, barely containing tears of relief as he convulses in a traumatic release. But then four knocks are heard, occurring off-camera, and he is suddenly still: knocking four times has been associated with the prophesied Doctor's demise throughout the two-part special episodes.

Another character, Wilf (Bernard Cribbins) is knocking on the glass door of a radiation chamber and, eventually, the Doctor will rescue him by absorbing all of that fatal energy in an adjoining chamber and releasing him. The Doctor describes this as his 'honour' but not before delivering a speech imbued with contrasting sentiments. Wilf implores the Doctor to leave him, an old man who's 'had his time,' and he replies:

'Well, exactly. Look at you. Not remotely important. But me? I could do so much more. So. Much. More! But this is what I get. My reward. Well, it's not fair!'

Figure 5.5 Doctor Who.

The words directed to Wilf are clearly insincere as, despite the sharpness of tone, there is never really the suggestion that he will leave him to die. But, when the Doctor shifts the focus upon himself, we are presented with a display of genuine anger and frustration. He paces around, shouts out with his head tilted upwards, beats his chest with his hands, and, finally, sweeps an array of objects onto the floor from the surface he leans upon. This fury emanates not so much from an acknowledgement of his cyclical burden, although a trace of that exists in his dutiful attachment to Wilf's predicament, but in an awareness that this sequence will somehow continue without 'him' – that changing form but retaining consciousness is an unjust existential disruption. This attitude contrasts with sentiments expressed later by the twelfth Doctor: rather than resisting the prospect of eternal continuity, the tenth Doctor articulates a desire for it to endure without change, and with his current identity unaltered. Camus' concept of Sisyphean happiness is hardly incorporated in this outlook and, indeed, we are left instead with the character's bitterness at being absent from the unending task. In this respect, we might reflect that the tenth Doctor has become inextricably bound to his burden to the extent that his compulsion to continue renders the prospect of any kind of withdrawal impossibly undue in his mind.

The Doctor's actions, once he has rescued Wilf and absorbed the lethal radiation, are therefore significant. He says that he is going to claim his 'reward' (linking back to his earlier speech) and then embarks on a journey that features visits to a series of former companions and associates. All of these involve elements of altruistic assistance and caretaking, ranging from literally saving the lives of some characters, to contriving a romantic liaison between others, to engineering a future lottery win, to simply checking that a now-deceased acquaintance had a happy life. Only the final encounter, with former companion Rose (Billie Piper) seems designed to provide the Doctor with a final 'rewarding' glimpse of a treasured friend. A sense is created, therefore, of this character revisiting figures from his life as the tenth incarnation of the Doctor in part to facilitate his own emotional return but also a means of reprising the role he has played for those years, to carry on saving people and striving to improve their lives. It is as though this behaviour is embedded so firmly that it dictates his choices at a profound level, guiding the way in which he chooses to engage with old friends, and constructing a responsibility that he struggles to relinquish. In each of the encounters, he rarely displays any hint of pleasure and, instead, is impassive or even morose. Again, we would struggle to find a trace of Camus' happy Sisyphus and, instead, might find that, in these moments, the Doctor possesses the face that Camus describes, so close to the stone that it has become stone itself. Indeed, in the Sisyphean context, the Doctor has developed a deeply-fused relationship with his position and his burden: his physical, emotional, and intellectual state shaped intensely by the conditions of an ever-repeating task. He is tied to it, as Sisyphus is bound by his rock, and his final words before regeneration express the extent to which the role has become his existence: 'I don't want to go.'[4] For this Doctor, leaving means ending, which is anathema to someone who is bonded so fundamentally to his burden. And, here, we might realise that the absence of pleasure in his behaviour now merely emphasises the satisfaction that he has drawn previously from his continual incumbrance, and which he is so reluctant to give up now. Like Camus' Sisyphus, he has indeed found happiness in his toil and fears the loss of both.

Resurrection of duty, therefore, is equated with the rediscovery of happiness. This is the trajectory that the eleventh Doctor's first episode must plot following the tenth's regeneration: to find a way back and restore its protagonist within the cycle. In the episode's climax, the Doctor makes a point of climbing to the roof of a hospital building, ascending the summit in an appropriate evocation of Sisyphean progress. There, he confronts the current threat to Earth's existence, the Atraxi (a kind of giant eyeball suspended on floating crystal-like shards), adopting reason and logic by asking whether this world is a threat, or whether its people are guilty of any crime under Atraxi laws. With negative answers to both, the Earth is saved. The Doctor, however, does not finish there and, instead, asks a further question:

> One more, just one. Is this world protected? Because you're not the first lot to have come here. Oh, there have been *so* many. And what you've got to ask is: what happened to them? Hello. I'm the Doctor. Basically, run.

The Atraxi has been projecting images in a kind of glowing orb up to this point and, in the first part of this speech, it displays a series of alien threats that the Doctor has faced over the years, including iconic figures like Cyberman, Daleks, and Sontarans. Their inclusion here perhaps secures viewer recognition, as even those without detailed knowledge of the show's history can pick out some recognisable elements. And, of course, these same foes keep returning again and again over episodes and seasons, never truly defeated and perennially contributing to the cycle of perpetual repetition: *becoming* that cycle. When the Doctor moves onto the question of what happened to these threats, the Atraxi projects images of all the previous incarnations of the Doctors, from first to tenth. The musical underscore, which has been building emphatically in pace and volume throughout this sequence reaches its tumultuous crescendo as the full orchestra of instruments is accompanied by an array of layered choral voices. The eleventh Doctor concludes his speech by stepping through the projected vision of the tenth, taking his place as the next incarnation within the line.

Figure 5.6 Doctor Who.

This scene marks a point of emphasis within the episode, and we can consider what themes are made prominent through aesthetic depiction. The alignment of words and images makes clear that this Doctor finds strength and purpose precisely through acknowledging his place within a wider cycle of repeating threats and accomplishments. The Atraxi. simply represent the latest in a never-ending barrage of enemies that must be overcome but, equally, this Doctor represents the latest in a series of Doctors that have embraced the task. The triumph and joy evoked in the line 'Basically, run' (and Smith's delivery of it) underscores the fact that the character has been restored: returned from the somewhat dark introspection that defined aspects of the tenth's departure. Through the show's audio-visual handling of the moment, that triumph and joy are related intrinsically to an acknowledgment of the repetition inherent within his existence: that this pattern will continue just as it has done before ('there have been *so* many'). And, crucially, this Doctor recognises that he is but one component within that cycle – one incarnation of a figure that has already taken many forms. This marks a reversal of the tenth's fleeting claim for exceptionalism ('I could do so much more. So much more'), stressing his reclamation of a Sisyphean role, and revealing the fulfilment this provides.

Notes

1 It seems that Praed's departure and Connery's succession were well-publicised, and so the withholding of the latter's identity in this episode would not appear to be teasing the idea that the former was continuing in the role.
2 In the 'new' era, regeneration has also triggered the destruction and renewal of the TARDIS interior, adding a further element of recapitulation to the process.
3 The brief evocation of the Tenth Doctor musical theme possesses a further meaning as it offers a reminder of Murray Gold's distinguished work as composer on all seasons of the 'new' *Doctor Who* up to this point. This episode marks the end of his tenure, and so a further point of transition – another farewell – is incorporated into the scene's aesthetic textures.
4 It should be noted that this regeneration also involved the changeover from one showrunner, Russell T Davies, to another, Steven Moffat. Whether the sentiment expressed by the Doctor echoed Davies' own view is debatable, but he would eventually return to the role of showrunner on *Doctor Who* in 2022, just as David Tennant has reprised his tenth Doctor on occasions. This at least creates interesting resonances within the final line written by Davies, performed by Tennant, and spoken by the Doctor.

6   Repetition and Revelation

This final chapter explores in greater detail the potential for repetition to be incorporated by shows as a means of exploring character-centred revelations. In each of the shows discussed, these revelations are related to what might broadly be termed the psychological perspectives of the central characters. It is worth noting that breadth, given that this work is in no way intended to function as a psychoanalytic study, which would self-evidently require specific training and expertise (although fields such as psychoanalysis have undoubtedly influenced the way other disciplines view and discuss psychological perspectives). How these psychological revelations are explored and expressed is a specific point of interest. There is a tendency in scholarly writing on television to separate aesthetic style from narrative structure, and this might be related to the wider practice of dividing form and content. In film studies, the drawbacks inherent in that kind of division are countered extensively in the work of V.F. Perkins and, specifically, in his chapter entitled '"How" is "What"' from the seminal book, *Film as Film* (Perkins 1972, 116–133). And in television studies, Jeremy Butler rejects the view of style as a 'flourish somehow layered on top of the narrative' when setting out the arguments in his influential volume, *Television Style* (Butler 2010, 15). Following those kinds of leads, this chapter is interested in the connections between the way something is shown and what is being told and, in turn, how decisions regarding narrative structure intrinsically shape stylistic presentation. In this way, part of this chapter's aim is to explore repetition as it features within an interrelationship between form and content within the shows discussed.

This is Going to Hurt

This is Going to Hurt (BBC 2022, hereafter *TIGTH*) is a drama that centres upon Adam (Ben Wishaw), an obstetrician working in a British hospital within the National Health Service (NHS). By the final episode of the series, Adam is experiencing significant trauma that can be associated with

DOI: 10.4324/9781003265283-7

a series of specific events that have affected him and, furthermore, emanates from a more general but equally pervasive situation that he is caught within. Acute examples might be found in his guilt over his poor treatment of a patient, which resulted in the premature delivery of her baby and a complaint being filed against Adam; an anonymous complaint about his professional conduct that was made by a colleague; and the very recent tragic death by suicide of a junior doctor, Shruti (Ambika Mod), towards whom Adam had adopted a harsh and unforgiving attitude. The broader context, however, involves the intrinsic nature of a professional environment that places intolerable physical and psychological burdens upon staff working within the NHS. Adam's job, which constantly demands his time and attention, effectively destroys all opportunities for a social life of any kind, leaves him dangerously deprived of sleep and impacts upon his mental health. The potential consequences of these pressures have already been exposed in the death of Shruti, which also emphasised the weight of expectation placed upon healthcare staff in a profession where perceptions and, indeed, definitions of success are tied fundamentally to critical patient care.

Depictions of this kind have a legacy in British medical dramas. In his 2003 book, *Body Trauma*, Jason Jacobs details the disillusionment that was growing among junior and senior doctors in the 1990s and early 2000s, resulting from the expansion of a managerial culture within the NHS coupled with various government measures that placed ever-increasing demands upon staff and instigated a decline in working standards (Jacobs 2003, 82–85). He provides a detailed account of the show *Cardiac Arrest* (BBC 1994–1996), illustrating its thoughtful but bitter and cynical response to the crisis, which distinguished it from other medical dramas that were broadcast at the time, such as *Casualty* (BBC 1986–) and *Peak Practice* (ITV 1993–2002). Jacobs quotes from an interview he conducted with *Cardiac Arrest*'s creator, Jed Mercurio:

> I think it was good that we had those programmes to contrast with – they distinguished us. We were really distinctive compared to them, we were the only one that injected a constant cynicism that permeated the series without any redemptive payoff – in other programmes doctors can be pissed-off but they see a baby born and are cured of their malaise. *Cardiac Arrest* was a reaction to these shows, it was very angry. And it was really a reaction to the smugness of other programme-makers who talked about how realistic their programmes were, but who didn't have a fucking clue.
>
> (Jacobs 2003, 89)

It is perhaps worth noting that *TIGTH* emphatically avoids the conventional cliché of a baby's birth signalling the lifting of a 'pissed-off' doctor's malaise, given that those working in the maternity ward are suffering extensively from profound difficulties caused by their working environment. Nevertheless, the show can be seen to share *Cardiac Arrest*'s ambition, as expressed by Mercurio, to provide a reaction whose anger and cynicism are rooted in a desire to give a more 'realistic' account of working life in the NHS. If both shows strive for authenticity, this may well derive from the professional backgrounds of their creators: both Mercurio and *TIGTH*'s writer Adam Kay were previously doctors and, in Kay's case, the television production was adapted from his bestselling autobiographical account.

With these distinctions in place, it is useful to consider how *TIGTH* depicts its central character both thematically and stylistically, as it attempts to provide a realistic exploration of his profound turmoil. Given the interests of this book, it is perhaps unsurprising to suggest that repetition features within this portrayal. However, unlike some other examples discussed already, we might hesitate to propose that repetition is the prominent feature of Adam's existence. Indeed, his professional life is defined emphatically by unexpected incidents and spontaneous challenges. Within the show, as in life, no two pregnancies follow the exact same course (with often dramatic divergences). It is notable that, in episode six when Adam takes a shift at a private maternity clinic, the atmosphere of predictable, managed calm is exposed as a façade when it turns out the facility cannot respond to an unforeseen medical emergency (a new mother is bleeding heavily) and the situation turns rapidly to a crisis. So, while the surface rhythms and routines of Adam's professional life may have the feel of repetition, from the continual churn of arriving at work already exhausted to the seemingly perpetual turnover of scrubs soiled by patients' bodily fluids to the perennial sonic intrusions of the electronic pager, the actual tasks he is required to perform bear the hallmarks of variation and diversity. It is the case, however, that these duties place an immense strain upon him.

So, rather than repetition necessarily becoming a central facet of Adam's professional existence, it is found instead in the camera's relationship to the show's central character and, particularly, the ways in which he is framed within his environment. We can stay with the final episode of the series to explore how this compositional pattern manifests. The episode opens with Adam visiting patients and performing procedures as he carries out his daily duties. As he leaves one room that two pregnant patients are having to share due to shortages, the camera tracks from behind as he walks through the corridors. Adam is framed centrally, in focus, while the surrounding details remain out of focus, making his physical form distinct within the spatial environment.

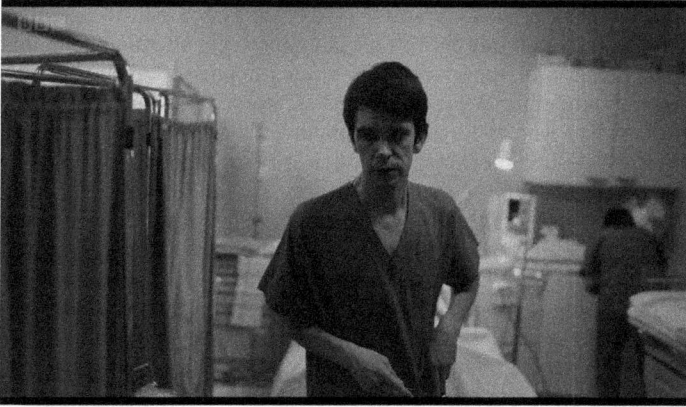

Figure 6.1 This is Going to Hurt.

Moments later, he is delivering a baby in another room and, having handed the newborn to mother, he moves across to look at the patient's notes. We cut to a low-angle shot of him as he reads and, again, he is positioned within the centre of the frame, in sharp focus, with both foreground and background details out of focus. A point-of-view shot of Shruti's signature on the notes triggers a series of flashback images recalling scenes they shared before we return again to the same shot of Adam as he reads. His thoughts are interrupted as the attending nurse has to deal with the patient's intoxicated partner urinating against the wall of the room but, in a reverse-medium shot that captures Adam's impassive response (as though he were still partially lost in his reflections, or that this kind of event is no longer surprising to him), he is once again framed centrally, in focus, with his surroundings blurred. In the early moments of the episode, a compositional pattern is becoming distinct, and it continues when Adam interacts with his colleagues. In the following scene, he speaks with a nurse, Ria (Philippa Dunne), and a junior doctor, Al (George Somner), who are both seated behind the main desk in the ward. Within the short conversation, we return three times to medium shots of Adam and, in each, he is framed in a similar style to previous scenes: located centrally within the *mise-en-scene*, in focus, with everything else appearing out of focus. As he engages in a new discussion with Al, the pattern continues, and as he walks away down the corridor in reverse shot, and again when he checks his buzzing phone.

With barely two minutes of the episode elapsed, the show demonstrates a repetitive and almost relentless predisposition to a particular style of framing, which it employs primarily but not exclusively in relation to Adam (other characters are sometimes portrayed in this way, as will be discussed in due course). To a significant extent, this compositional strategy not only encourages but even forces attention upon this character's physical appearance and, related implicitly to this, his psychological condition. What do we see? A worn out, cynical, deflated, unshaven man who is forced to respond over and over again to the circumstances unfolding before him. Ben Wishaw possesses a particular gentleness of vocal tone that underscores even Adam's most acerbic remarks and angry outbursts with a brittle vulnerability, emphasising that his character is damaged even as he ostensibly damages others. Similarly, while he delivers world-weary, withering looks and rolls his eyes in response to others, Wishaw's physical manner has a diminutive, almost child-like, quality (his slim frame resembling a pre-adolescent who has not yet 'filled out') that has the capacity to elicit sympathy. Wishaw balances these contrasting qualities within his performance, and the show's style of depiction gives emphasis to the contrasts he shapes. The framing pattern extends not only across the scenes mentioned, but the whole episode and, indeed, the entirety of the show's seven episodes. *TIGHT* revisits the same visual motif again and again, reminding us continuously of this character's traits and idiosyncrasies.

This central framing pattern also has a legacy, however, that can be related to trends found within cinema. In a landmark article, Jeffrey Sconce notes that a type of cinema he describes as 'smart' – not quite 'art' cinema, 'Hollywood' cinema or, technically, 'independent' cinema (Sconce 2002, 351) – possesses certain common aesthetic strategies, including something he terms 'blank style' (Ibid, 359). Discussing blank style, Sconce gives the example of Todd Haynes' *Safe* (1995) and, in a

Figure 6.2 This is Going to Hurt.

note accompanying a series of still images from the film, observes that the director 'often places a hapless Carol (Julianne Moore) centre-frame and alone in the midst of static mise-en-scene' (Ibid). This relates to Sconce's wider point that blank style often involves 'the frequent (even dominant) use of long-shots, static composition, and sparse cutting' (Ibid), but his perception of central framing within *Safe* isolates a specific feature that can be found across works that might fall within his definition (in the films of director Wes Anderson, for example). The observation of this pattern occurs again in related work such as James MacDowell's study of 'quirky' cinema (which acknowledges a relationship to Sconce's concept) as he draws attention to the central framing of characters in the films *Punch Drunk Love* (Paul Thomas Anderson 2002), *Buffalo 66* (Vincent Gallo 1998) and *Napoleon Dynamite* (Jared Hess 2004). MacDowell places this stylistic commonality within a broader tendency for 'quirky' films to feature 'static, flat-looking, medium-long or long shots that feel nearly geometrically even, depicting isolated or carefully arranged characters, sometimes facing directly out towards us, who are made to look faintly ridiculous or out-of-place by virtue of the composition's rigidity' (MacDowell 2010: 6).

The stylistic tendencies of films from the 1990s and 2000s that Sconce and MacDowell identify respectively, which includes the consistent central framing of characters, can also be found in subsequent television shows. Jessica Ford proposes a direct relationship between the US series *Girls* (HBO 2012–17) and the concept of 'smart' film (Ford 2016) whilst, in the UK, it is worth noting that one of *TIGTH*'s directors, Lucy Forbes, and one of its cinematographers, Benedict Spence, worked on *The End of the Fxxxing World* (Channel 4/Netflix 2017–2019), a show that exhibits many of the characteristics that both Sconce and MacDowell mention. In terms of Sconce's argument, not only does it possess similar stylistic traits but its tone and narrative shape also encompasses an engagement with themes of irony and nihilism that he regards as central to 'smart' cinema. *TIGTH*'s relationship to those aspects is more remote however: while characters may express degrees of nihilistic reflection and the comedic tone of some scenes can be described as ironic (with the concession that it is a notoriously elusive and contested term[1]), this is balanced against a hospital workplace environment that has sincerity and purpose as principal attributes. The distinctions between *TIGTH* and Sconce's characterisation of 'smart' cinema extend to questions of aesthetic form, as Sconce maintains that blank style 'cultivates a sense of distance in the audience' and 'produces tension through dividing audience and storyworld [...] as a means of fostering a sense of clinical observation' (Sconce, 360). *TIGHT*'s consistent use of direct address perhaps self-evidently works against the kind of distance and divide that Sconce describes, creating an overt point of connection between viewer and character. However, even the consistent central framing of Adam within the show appears more complex. It certainly emphasises his separation from his surrounding environment to a degree, and this is further accentuated as those details are regularly out of focus in contrast to his presentation. But the continual return to this visual composition – extending across seven forty-five-minute episodes – also has the effect of reinforcing again and again a relationship between character and audience: we are repeatedly drawn into an appreciation of his emotional and intellectual condition as he is made especially prominent within the *mise-en-scene*. Our observation of him, therefore, might well be more compassionate than 'clinical.'

The repeated centre-frame depiction of Adam is revelatory. It occurs not only within the setting of his hospital workplace but elsewhere in other locations: in the final episode he is framed this way in a café, his parents' house, and a wedding reception, for example. This physical dislocation from his surroundings thus becomes a pervasive element of his entire life as it is represented onscreen, symbolising an emotional distance that he has developed and, possibly, cultivated as a coping strategy (combining with an innate social awkwardness that the show attributes partially to his overbearing and demanding mother). The pattern persists within a sequence occurring towards the end of the episode, when Adam and ex-boyfriend Harry (Rory Fleck Byrne) have fled a wedding reception and jumped into a nearby lake. As they bob in the water, Adam reflects upon the breakdown of their relationship, suggesting: 'the bad stuff ... that was all to do with my job. Medicine's not good for me. It's ruined my life. And it destroyed us.' Harry replies 'I don't think it was that simple ...' before we cut to Adam at his misconduct tribunal. This returns us to a point from earlier in the episode, where Adam had broken protocol to stand up and make a speech. Before, the show made available the possibility that he had followed the advice of his senior, Mr Lockhart (Alex Jennings), and blamed Shruti for the error that led to a profoundly ill patient being sent home from the hospital. (The further events of the tribunal were not shown and we simply learned that its outcome had not led to Adam being struck off.) As the scene resumes, however, Adam instead gives a true account of Shruti's death, the unbearable pressures she faced, and the impossible burden placed on a profession in which 'one doctor, in this country, takes their own life every three weeks.' It is a powerful speech, which the show interweaves with the scene at the lake as Adam begins to propose leaving medicine so that he can commit properly to a relationship with Harry, joining together the tribunal testimony and his speculation about new horizons.

Perhaps inevitably, Adam is framed centrally at both the lake and the tribunal. Harry is also depicted in this style (with background details similarly out of focus in his shots) and there is a sense of him being drawn into Adam's thoughts and emotions through their sympathetic relationship as he temporarily shares a style of physical depiction within the frame. The show places dramatic tension upon Adam's words as he considers two alternative existences. Indeed, the episode has offered brief evocations of different lives he might pursue: cradling a baby with the care and love of a new father in one scene and, later, looking down the aisle of the wedding as he hopes to see Harry, just after the bride-to-be has walked past, as though searching for his own future husband. Finally, however, when Harry says 'Being a doctor, it's who you are. Put your hand on your heart and tell me you want to give all that up,' shots of Adam are intercut with shots of babies, patients, and colleagues as he recalls meaningful and poignant moments at work. He replies, 'I don't think I can,' and the couple embrace in the water: centrally-framed in medium-long shot with the surrounding trees and lake out of focus, Harry's head placed in front of Adam's, as though they had merged and momentarily become one physical entity. Given the context of the discussion between them, this point of sympathetic embrace also marks the beginning of an eventual parting, as Adam has chosen his profession over their relationship. Harry shares completely the physical positioning that has characterised Adam's portrayal throughout the series, but this surely will not be sustained. When Adam makes his choice, we can perhaps appreciate that the isolation he maintains from his world, necessitated by his work and emphasised persistently in the show's physical depiction of his character, is embedded intrinsically and to such a degree that he cannot escape it. As the show returns to the same composition over and over again, it reinforces this truth through repetition. As much as Adam's separation is a product of his working environment, it also emanates from him and, ultimately, he is willing to embrace this as a major facet of his existence. The show's style of composition has offered this revelation consistently throughout the episodes, constantly returning to that centre-framed shot of Adam and, in doing so, proposing separation, distance, and isolation to be natural instincts for him: an innate quality that re-emerges continuously.

The conclusion of *TIGTH*, therefore, possesses an ambiguous tone. Adam returns to his job and, in a final scene, he delivers a baby in the hospital car park before his shift has even begun. In one sense, this illustrates his noble dedication to an important profession, continuing his crucial contribution to society. However, we would perhaps struggle to balance this against an awareness of the pressure that work exerts upon him and the impact it has on his capacity to interact meaningfully with his world, as emphasised so relentlessly within the show's repeated visual composition. Indeed, as Adam walks away from the scene of the impromptu car park delivery, he is once again framed centrally, a remote

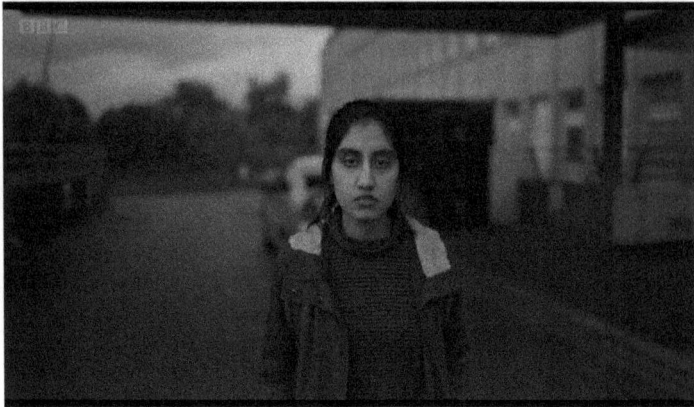

Figure 6.3 This is Going to Hurt.

figure adrift within his out-of-focus surroundings. We might recall Shruti, who tragically succumbed to these intolerable circumstances. Our last view of her, as she delivered the chilling words 'I'm sorry. I really did try' directly to the camera, was in a shot that framed her centrally, with background details blurred.

The graphic resemblance between this moment and Adam's style of depiction throughout the show reminds us of the instability that is a defining feature of the profession: that choosing a life of dedication can have profound consequences for the health of doctors, nurses, and everyone working in the NHS. The style of framing makes clear that the risk is still there for Adam: as he returns to his car to find that he has received a parking fine while delivering the baby in another vehicle, centrally framed in medium shot, surroundings out of focus, his future is left precarious.

I May Destroy You

In its penultimate episode, Michaela Coel's *I May Destroy You* (BBC 2020)[2] might at first be seen to offer a series of potential resolutions, each of which vary from character to character as they individually cope with the trauma and abuse they have suffered. Terry (Weruche Opia) has finally gained an acting job for a TV commercial and is in the early stages of a new relationship with Kai (Tyler Luke Cunningham), who has to explain to her that two men she took to be strangers were actually accomplices who abused her by tricking her into a threesome months ago. Kwarme (Paapa Essiedu) was sexually assaulted in an earlier episode and received no support when he reported the crime to the police. The assault left him feeling unsafe dating men, and so he disastrously initiated a sexual encounter with a woman, Nilufer (Pearl Chanda), before resuming his prolific use of the Grindr application. In this episode, however, he has met with Nilufer to explain his actions and apologise (which she doesn't accept), and has begun a meaningful relationship with a new partner, Tyrone (Gershwyn Eustache Jr.).

Finally, a central plotline of the series has involved Arabella (Coel) as she contends with twice being the survivor of rape: when she was assaulted after her drink was spiked on a night out and later when a sexual partner, Zain (Karan Gill) removed his condom during intercourse. The show weaves together various aspects of Arabella's life (now and from her past) alongside its portrayal of these crimes enacted against her and their aftermath. With her mental health profoundly affected, for example, she struggles to meet a deadline that her publishers impose for the writing of her next book and, when she seeks support from them, they show little empathy, and her contract is eventually cancelled.[3] In the penultimate episode, Arabella has accepted the help of Zain, who was originally supposed to support her writing, using it dispassionately to restructure and, consequently, reinvigorate her novel. In a sequence where the newly energised Arabella refashions her work by sticking an array of ordered post-it note plot details across her bedroom walls, 'It's Gonna Rain' by the Reverend Milton Brunson and The Thompson Community Singers plays on the soundtrack.

This song was used in the first episode of the series, underscoring a sequence in which Arabella suffers extreme disorientation and nausea, staggering and falling in a bar due to the drugs that were slipped into her drink prior to the premeditated rape she will be a victim of. The replaying of the song in this later scene creates a connection with that earlier use and also invites a comparison. We might recognise, for example, a difference between Arabella's position then, as someone who is about to be subjected to violent criminal abuse, and now, as she discovers a new purpose and direction, physically driven by her creative force. The song's first verse (the only one we hear in both scenes), and the ways in which we can interpret it, encapsulate this discrepancy, as it describes 'clouds gathering' and running to an ark 'before the rain starts.' Although 'It's Gonna Rain' is an expression of religious devotion, the show invites an association of its meanings with Arabella. In the bar scene, for example, we might view the oncoming storm described as a reflection of the horrifying offence that is about to be committed against her, with the safety of an 'ark' never reached (this lyric is heard as Arabella struggles to reach the doors that would lead away from the threat, but she doesn't make it through them). Whereas, in the bedroom scene, we see an Arabella

Figure 6.4 I May Destroy You.

who has transcended any literal connotations within the words, becoming her own storm as she builds her narrative with newfound momentum and, in the process, crafting an ark that will carry her through the torrent of memories that are positioned as points of inspiration as they appear onscreen in briefly-held snatches of flashback images. The song's repetition reveals change and, as with Terry and Kwarme, we might gain a sense of Arabella moving towards a kind of resolution.

The notion that the show is establishing this overall resolution evaporates suddenly when, in the final minutes of the episode, Arabella recognises the man who raped her (Lewis Reeves) and the man who was complicit (Chin Nyenwe). This recognition triggers in her a succession of memories from that night, whereas previously she had struggled to remember details due to the drugs she had unknowingly taken. This pivotal moment is represented in a sequence of scenes from that night, often but not exclusively from Arabella's perspective, and the show emphasises the importance of her revelation by repeating this sequence at the beginning of the final episode (*IMDY* does not usually recap moments from previous episodes). From here, events move quickly. Arabella takes Terry to the toilets where, confused and conflicted, she struggles to comprehend the situation. At first, Terry is more composed while Arabella is understandably erratic, but she slowly becomes calmer and focussed as she reveals to her friend that she has a long-held plan to 'hurt' him, and even has costumes to help facilitate the act. She explains that they are going to inject him with his own drugs and, after her initial shock, Terry commits to the plan.

Their friend, Theo (Harriet Webb) joins them in the bar: she steals the rapist's remaining stash of drugs while Arabella distracts him, and Terry likewise distracts his accomplice. The scheme works: the rapist (whose name, we learn, is Patrick) attempts to spike Arabella's drink but, unbeknown to him, she spits it out and tips it away. Following her convincing performance of being drugged, Patrick takes Arabella into the toilets and, in a cubicle, begins to assault her. But suddenly, she reveals that she is fully conscious, and Theo injects the drugs into his ankle from an adjacent cubicle. Arabella accentuates her new power over Patrick in this encounter, kissing him full on the mouth and then forcefully blocking the door when he attempts to leave. She lets him go but realises that he still has her underwear. The trio follows him through street after street until, finally, he collapses. They retrieve the underwear but Arabella declares that she wants to see Patrick's penis. As she achieves this, he wakes up and suddenly the scene turns to violence: Arabella punches him in the groin and then continues to punch him in the face and kick him while Theo chokes him with her underwear. With a final blow from Arabella, he is lifeless, and she must travel with his corpse propped up on the night bus before finally bundling it under her bed. She changes out of her entrapment guise and begins to write new notes for her bedroom wall, but Patrick's blood smears across them, and, looking down, she sees a dark red pool forming on the floor. She walks out of the bedroom.

We cut to Arabella sitting in the small outside courtyard of her flat. In close-up, she stares out and beyond the camera, as though lost in contemplation, and we might reasonably take this to be the morning after last night's ordeals.

Figure 6.5 *I May Destroy You.*

However, when her flatmate, Ben (Stephen Wight), enters the space through the kitchen window and they start repeating lines of dialogue from the previous evening, we realise that we have in fact somehow moved back in time and that evening has restarted. And yet, as small details are altered such as Ben entering the courtyard after Arabella and both delivering the lines slightly differently, this is revealed to be another version of that evening: similar, but not identical. Later in the bar, the pattern of events at first appears to repeat identically: Arabella recognising the rapist and going to the toilets with Terry. This time, however, it is Terry who takes control assertively, disclosing that she has a plan to entrap the criminal, whilst Arabella reacts with hesitancy and bemusement. They enact the plan: under Terry's direction, Arabella consumes a large quantity of cocaine, approaches the rapist (now called David in this scenario), and drinks the spiked gin and tonic he gives her (the stimulant drugs already in her system counteracting the tranquilising effects). Arabella pretends to be affected by the sedatives and staggers away from David: he takes hold of her and guides her to the toilets whilst, having observed these events, Terry calls the police. In a toilet cubicle, as David begins his assault, Arabella reveals that his sedative has not affected her and, at first, he acts violently and threateningly: grabbing her face and slamming her against a wall, bringing his face close against hers whilst attempting to demean her outrage and spewing a succession of misogynist insults. Arabella remains still, impassive and composed as she meets his gaze unflinchingly but, then, his sadism transitions into masochism as he directs the verbal abuse back towards himself, using his own name now and referring to sexual assaults committed against him. He breaks down in tears, his tense hold upon Arabella evolves into an embrace and, when the police arrive in a following scene, the couple have fled. She takes him to her bedroom and listens with extraordinary tenderness as he reveals details about his life and his crimes. Indeed, it is David who expresses unease with being allowed to sit on her bed and, just before the police arrive to take him away, she warmly embraces him. When he is gone, she suppresses a sob before tearing some paper in half to make two new notes, which she sticks to her bedroom wall. The scene cuts.

We are back in the small courtyard, the evening about to begin again, and the same conversation between Arabella and Ben. This time, though, it is altered through a shortening of the exchanges as we move swiftly into the bar scene, where Arabella's identification of the rapist is similarly truncated. In this version of events, however, she does not share the recognition with Terry and, instead, approaches him (now called Patrick, again) and instigates a passionate kiss in a toilet cubicle, followed by sexual intercourse in her bedroom. Their sex builds up to Arabella penetrating Patrick, bringing him to orgasm, in a transcending of conventional roles that was prefigured in the bar as Patrick's accomplice performed the lap-dance for Terry that she previously delivered for him. The following morning, after they have woken up, Patrick tells Arabella 'I'm not going to go unless you tell me to' and she replies 'Go.' He leaves, naked, followed by the 'dead Patrick' from a previous version of the evening, who emerges from under her bed carrying a bag containing items from an earlier abortion that she had also stored there. Arabella is left alone and, as the front door slams shut, she sighs and looks up at her bedroom wall. We cut to a shot of one particular note, posted between many, that reads simply: 'Garden – Ben.' Arabella points at it, before taking it along with the next note in the sequence, and leaves the room.

We are back in the courtyard garden. Ben repeats a line heard in all the other versions of this scene: 'That is such a loud bird' but, this time, Arabella listens and responds: 'Hmm? I wonder where it's coming from?' And, this time, she does not go to the bar to continue her vigil: after giving Ben an impromptu hug, she decides to stay at home with him.

This is a final version of that evening's events, defining all of the others as works of imagination. In a key article on *IMDY*, Caetlin Benson-Allott writes that 'Every ending precludes other, and none reverses the harm done' (Benson-Allott 2020, 105) and, indeed, this final scenario marks an acceptance that no form of assertive action – going to the bar and experiencing various confrontations – could ever reverse the harm, thus not only precluding those earlier versions as actual occurrences but also precluding them as meaningful options. The repeating of the evening's events within these different configurations can certainly be read as Arabella's working through of her trauma, conforming to a recognised Freudian

Figure 6.6 I May Destroy You.

model. We might also note that she engages in a particularly creative type of repetition, trying out different narrative scenarios as an attempt to process her pain. This aligns with Arabella's status as a writer, and the repeated motif of her constructing and re-ordering the notes on her bedroom wall evokes the sense of her putting together a narrative, testing different components to form a complete story.

This can be expanded if we consider Coel's overarching role as the creator of each scenario and the overall fictional landscape. Benson-Allott suggests that 'By combining multiple opportunities for catharsis within a single episode, Coel offers such an abundance of closure that viewers can appreciate how ambivalent the concept really is' (Ibid). In the first three versions of events, Arabella seeks catharsis through action and each approach relies upon a form of engagement with her assailant: giving him a face, name, identity, and even history. The rapist, therefore, occupies a centralised position within Arabella's process of working through, which in itself resembles certain types of media narratives circulating more broadly: the criminal as the target of a sensational rape revenge drama; the criminal with a fascinating and complex psychological history; or the criminal who is capable of both appalling violence and sensual affection. In each of these configurations, the aggressor is kept in focus to various extents within stories that create dramatic intrigue around that figure. Arabella's pursuit of the rapist in each storyline might, on the surface, begin to conform with those kinds of narratives but, as Coel effectively discards each of the options, she also rejects the notion that Arabella's situation can have that kind of conventional resolution, which might be found elsewhere in media representations of crime, and which often risks diluting a focus upon the victim by incorporating the criminal as a point of interest. The show's recapitulation of the same evening reinforces and intensifies Coel's rejection of the ways in which this story might be told and, crucially, resolved. Each potential forking path is closed off with every reset until we are left with a more ambiguous conclusion: Ben disappears into the kitchen and Arabella is left gazing across the courtyard. Resolution or, indeed, catharsis are not fixed ideas in this moment and, rather than being brought to the surface as they are so dramatically in the alternative versions of events, they remain private to Arabella, existing on her terms.

The repeated re-fashioning of the evening also makes clear that an ideal endpoint may not exist in this story. Each scenario resists an entirely rewarding or comforting outcome for Arabella, and each contains elements that are unsettling and difficult. In this way, their arrangement within a repeating structure emphasises the idea that any attempt to depict the aftermath of rape may not conform to ideas of narrative closure, with each ending simply replaced by the next. As Arabella sits in the courtyard in the final scenario, she looks out into a future that is uncertain and precarious. How she contends with the abuse she has suffered is not a settled matter and her new perspective may represent the beginning of a journey rather than an end.[4] That will also involve acknowledging absence: the fact that the police investigation has found no suspects for her rape. As Coel reinvents new identities for the rapist each time, she also underpins the truth that this figure cannot be identified in Arabella's real life. In one sense, this maintains a useful focus on Arabella, resisting the ways in which the criminal can sometimes become a point of interest in media narratives, as discussed earlier. However, it also represents a more realistic telling of this story. In 2020, 52,210 rapes were recorded by police in England and Wales, yet only 843 resulted in a charge or a summons: a rate of 1.6% (Barr and Topping 2021). This is not to say, of course, that the identity of the rapist is unknown, as it is Arabella's case. However, as the show repeatedly discards each new dramatisation of her imagined re-encounter with the rapist, it arrives at a portrayal that reflects perhaps more accurately the experiences of many survivors in the UK, for whom catharsis cannot be found within the criminal justice system.[5] Therefore, within a cycle of recapitulation, the show explores Arabella's fantasised alternative retributions and resolutions in light of this absence before returning to a reality in which such conclusions can never be realised.

Notes

1 James MacDowell's *Irony in Film* (2016) provides an extensive consideration of this theme.
2 Coel wrote, co-directed (with Sam Miller) and co-executive produced (with Phil Clarke, Roberto Troni, Sam Miller and Jo McLellan) the show.
3 Arabella's publisher does pay for a counselling session, which she attends, and employs another author to help with the writing of the novel. Given their otherwise unsympathetic responses, it is hard not to see these gestures of support as transactions, the costs of which are balanced against the lucrative potential of future book sales. Equally, it is suggested that Zain had some sort of reputation for inappropriateness within the publishing industry, and so the decision to have him help Arabella may represent a dubious duty of care on the part of her publishers.
4 The publication of Arabella's next book is depicted, after an implied passage of time, as a standalone achievement, rather than a means of working through her trauma. The book's content is not revealed.
5 It is important to note that Kwarme's sexual assault is not even recorded by the police, as he is met with far less empathy and professional rigour when he reports it.

Conclusion

This book has attempted to place an emphasis upon repetition in the study of television, suggesting that it can be a productive feature in conceptualisations of the medium and, furthermore, that individual shows engage with and employ the theme skilfully and imaginatively. As a result, the discussion has implicitly connected repetition with achievement in television. These kinds of efforts are, in part, intended as a response to certain negative associations that repetition can sometimes evoke, as discussed in the introduction and chapter two, especially in relation to television. Whilst understandable (because repetition *can* be tedious, monotonous, and unimaginative, for example) these perceptions nevertheless have the potential to inhibit any sustained consideration of the theme. This book has, therefore, begun to explore some of the ways in which repetition might be valued as a feature of television specifically, and speculate upon how this could enrich our understanding and appreciation of certain shows.

It perhaps goes without saying that a book containing six main case studies is not intended to be an exhaustive or, indeed, conclusive account. On the contrary, in common perhaps with all academic studies, this book is intended to invite further reflection and encourage future debate. Although my discussion does take in different types of programming, repetition permeates through a wide range of television content and there are certainly opportunities to move beyond any parameters set out within this current study. Likewise, while different related media are referenced briefly in chapter one of the book, providing a foundation for the focus on television, I am sure that there is existing work on repetition in films, music, and video games, for example, that I am unaware of and that these areas might equally be explored further in future studies.

If the chapters within this book build towards the notion that repetition can have value in the study of television, we might turn to a broader question of what value repetition within television could bring to viewers. I suspect that we would, with some justification, resist the idea that television can reliably provide us with advice and direction for our everyday lives. Most shows are surely not designed or equipped for that kind of intervention and, furthermore, every individual's experiences are particular to such a degree that no text could hope to adequately address the span of its audience. Nevertheless, each of the shows offered as case studies in this book involve characters contending with, negotiating, indulging in, celebrating, harnessing or utilising facets of repetition within their lives (and, doubtless, there are forms of interaction that extend beyond the list I have provided here). Undeniably, repetition features in all our lives, albeit in different forms and to various degrees. It is all around us, running through our experiences and guiding our thoughts and actions. Repetition can evoke disparate reactions within us, ranging from comfort and security to frustration and despondency. Consequently, shows that centre upon and creatively employ types of repetition can be seen to form a connection, however tenuous, with the lives of viewers, finding points of resonance and maybe potential resemblance. They are hardly self-help guides, but they do encapsulate aspects of a shared experience. We are not celebrity restaurant reviewers, or NHS doctors, or time travellers, but we might find that some facets of those lives touch our own, however lightly and however briefly. And I am compelled to suggest that one important common feature, the thing we *all* have in common, is repetition.

References

Allen, Michael and Janet McCabe. 'Imitations of lives: vocal mimicry and performing celebrity in *The Trip*.' *Celebrity Studies* 3, no. 2 (2012): 150–163.

Ardehali, Rod. 'BBC boss sparks outrage after claiming viewers "love repeats" at Christmas – as it emerges over two-thirds of festive content BBC 1 and 2 has been aired before.' *MailOnline*. 8 December 2018. https://www.dailymail.co.uk/news/article-6474263/BBC-boss-sparks-outrage-claiming-viewers-love-repeats-Christmas.html

Barr, Caelainn and Alexandra Topping. 'Fewer than 1 in 60 rape cases lead to charge in England and Wales.' *The Guardian*. 23 May 2021. https://www.theguardian.com/society/2021/may/23/fewer-than-one-in-60-cases-lead-to-charge-in-england-and-wales

Bellour, Raymond. 'Cine-repetitions.' *Screen* 20, no. 2 (Summer 1979): 65–72.

Benson-Allott, Caetlin. 'How *I May Destroy You* reinvents rape television.' *Film Quarterly* 74, no. 2 (2020): 100–105.

Brunsdon, Charlotte. 'Bingeing on Box-Sets: The national and the digital in television crime drama.' In *Relocating Television: Television in the Digital Context*, edited by Jostein Gripsrud, 63–75. Oxon: Routledge, 2010.

Bryan, Scott. 'Repeat viewing: why the past is the future of our TV schedules.' *The Guardian*. 21 July 2020. https://www.theguardian.com/tv-and-radio/2020/jul/21/tv-repeats-pandemic-london-2012-olympics-big-brother-society

Butler, Jeremy. *Television Style*. Oxon: Routledge, 2010.

Camus, Albert. *The Myth of Sisyphus*. London: Penguin Books, 2005. (translation first published 1955).

Cardwell, Sarah. 'Television aesthetics: Stylistic analysis and beyond.' In *Television Aesthetics and Style*, edited by Jason Jacob and Steven Peacock, 23–43. London: Bloomsbury, 2013.

Chapman, James. *Swashbucklers: The Costume Adventure Series*. Manchester: Manchester University Press, 2015.

Creeber, Glen, ed. *Fifty Key Television Programmes*. London: Bloomsbury, 2004.

Eco, Umberto. 'Innovation and repetition: between modern & postmodern aesthetics.' *Daedalus* 134, no. 4 (Fall 2005) (first published 1985): 191–207.

Ellis, John. *Visible Fictions: Cinema: Television: Video*. London: Routledge, 1997. [first published 1982].

Ellis, John. *Seeing Things: Television in the Age of Uncertainty*. London: I.B. Tauris, 2000.

Fiske, John and John Hartley. 1978. *Reading Television*. London: Methuen.

Ford, Jessica. 'The "smart" body politics of Lena Durnham's *Girls*.' *Feminist Media Studies* 16, no. 6 (Spring 2016): 1029–1042.

Geraghty, Christine. 'Aesthetics and quality in popular television drama.' *International Journal of Cultural Studies* 6, no. 1 (2003): 25–45.

'Great Canal Journeys.' Channel 4. Accessed 12 December 2022. https://www.channel4.com/programmes/great-canal-journeys

Grindon, Leger. 'Cycles and clusters: The shape of film genre history.' In *Film Genre Reader IV*, edited by Keith Barry Grant, 42–59. Austin: University of Texas Press, 2012.

Henderson, Stuart. *The Hollywood Sequel: History & Form, 1911–2010*. London: British Film Institute/Palgrave, 2014.

Hills, Matt. 'Television aesthetics: a pre-structuralist danger?' *Journal of British Cinema and Television* 8, no. 1 (2011): 99–117.

Holdsworth, Amy. *Television, Memory and Nostalgia*. Basingstoke: Palgrave, 2011.

Jacobs, Jason. 'Issues of judgement and value in television studies.' *International Journal of Cultural Studies* 4, no. 4 (2001): 427–447.

Jacobs, Jason. *Body Trauma: The New Hospital Dramas*. London: British Film Institute, 2003.

Jacobs, Jason. 'Television aesthetics: an infantile disorder.' *Journal of British Cinema and Television* 3, no. 1 (2006): 19–33.

Jacobs, Jason. and Steven Peacock, eds. *Television Aesthetics and Style*. London: Bloomsbury, 2013.

Jacobs, Jason. '*True detective* and practical criticism.' *CST Online*. 11 April 2014. https://cstonline.net/true-detective-and-practical-criticism-by-jason-jacobs/

Kawin, Bruce. *Telling It Again and Again: Repetition in Literature and Film*. London: Cornell University Press, 1972.

Klevan, Andrew. *Aesthetic Evaluation and Film*. Manchester: Manchester University Press, 2018.

Kompare, Derek. *Rerun Nation: How Repeats Invented American Television*. Oxon: Routledge, 2005.

Lavigne, Carlen and Heather Marcovitch, eds. *American Remakes of British Television: Transformations and Mistranslations*. Plymouth: Lexington Books, 2011.

Lavigne, Carlen, ed. *Remake Television: Reboot, Re-use, Recycle*. Plymouth: Lexington Books, 2014.

Leitch, Thomas. 'Adaptations without Sources: The adventures of Robin Hood.' *Literature/Film Quarterly* 36, no. 1 (2008): 21–30.

Levine, Alexandra S. 'How "Canon in D Major" Became the Wedding Song.' *New York Times*. 12 May 2019, sec. ST, 12.

MacDowell, James. 'Notes on quirky.' *Movie: A Journal of Film Criticism* 1 (August 2010). https://warwick.ac.uk/fac/arts/scapvc/film/movie/contents/notes_on_quirky.pdf

MacDowell, James. *Irony in Film*. London: Palgrave MacMillian, 2016.

McPherson, Tara. 'Horace Newcomb in conversation with Tara McPherson.' *E-Media Studies*. Summer 2007. https://journals.dartmouth.edu/cgi-bin/WebObjects/Journals.woa/xmlpage/4/article/320

Medhurst, Andy. *A National Joke: Popular Comedy and English Cultural Identities.* Oxon: Routledge, 2007.

Molina-Whyte, Lidia. 'Queen's funeral estimated to be watched by 37.5 million in the UK – 4 billion worldwide.' *Radio Times.* 21 September 2022. https://www. radiotimes.com/tv/current-affairs/queen-funeral-tv-viewers-worldwide-newsupdate/

Morris, Nigel. '"Do you like taster menus?" Beyond hybridity: *the Trip & The Trip to Italy.*' *New Review of Film and Television Studies* 20, no. 4 (2015): 422–442.

Newcomb, Horace. *TV: The Most Popular Art.* New York: Anchor Books/ Doubleday, 1974.

Ouelette, Laurie. *Lifestyle TV.* Oxon: Routledge, 2016.

Paglia, Camille. *Glittering Images: A Journey Through Art from Egypt to Star Wars.* New York: Vintage Books, 2013.

Perkins, V.F. *Film as Film: Understanding and Judging Movies.* Harmondsworth: Penguin, 1972.

Piper, Helen. 'Broadcast drama and the problem of television aesthetics: home, nation, universe.' *Screen* 57, no. 2 (2016): 163–183.

Sanjeck, David. 'Same as it ever was: Innovation and exhaustion in the horror and science fiction films of the 1990s.' In *Film Genre 2000: New Critical Essays*, edited byWheeler Winston Dixon, 111–124. Albany: State University of New York Press, 2000.

Sconce, Jeffrey. 'Irony, nihilism and the new American "smart" film.' *Screen* 43, no. 4 (Winter 2002): 349–369.

Silverstone, Roger. *Television and Everyday Life.* London: Routledge, 1994.

Taylor, Richard. *Good and Evil.* New York: Prometheus Books, 2000.

'Wedding string quartet – canon in D (Johann Pachelbel).' YouTube. Accessed 12 December 2022. https://www.youtube.com/watch?v=es_3F3TLJS0

Williams, Raymond. *Television: Technology and Cultural Form.* Oxon: Routledge, 2003. [first published 1974].

Zborowski, James. 'The presentation of detail and the organisation of time in *The Royle Family.*' In *Television Aesthetics and Style*, edited by Jason Jacobs and Steven Peacock 125–134. London: Bloomsbury, 2013.

Index

Note: *Italicized* page numbers refer to figures. Page numbers followed by "n" refer to notes.

For Product Safety Concerns and Information please contact our EU
representative GPSR@taylorandfrancis.com
Taylor & Francis Verlag GmbH, Kaufingerstraße 24, 80331 München, Germany

www.ingramcontent.com/pod-product-compliance
Lightning Source LLC
Chambersburg PA
CBHW061753270326
41928CB00011B/2487

9 781032 207988